Memories of
CHILDHOOD

COLLECTING
FOR PLEASURE

Memories of CHILDHOOD

BRACKEN BOOKS

Editor Dorothea Hall
Art Editor Gordon Robertson
Production Inger Faulkner

Concept, design and production by
Marshall Cavendish Books
119 Wardour Street
London W1V 3TD

This edition published 1992 by Bracken Books
an imprint of Studio Editions Limited,
Princess House, 50 Eastcastle Street
London W1N 7AP England

Typeset by Litho Link Ltd.
Printed and bound in Hong Kong

ISBN 1 85170 914 2

Some of this material was previously published in the Marshall Cavendish partwork *Times Past*

CONTENTS

INTRODUCTION

There is an undeniable aura of magic surrounding childhood things from any period in history. During the Victorian and Edwardian eras the growing realization that children were young people with individual needs and interests of their own served to inspire the creation of some of the most innovative toys and games (including furniture and artefacts) that have ever been made – many of which have survived today.

As with other antique-collecting enthusiasts, collectors of childhood memorabilia tend to specialize in certain areas favouring such items as teddy bears, bisque dolls, tin toys, train sets, comics, books and children's annuals. Other collectables with immense appeal are the scaled-down versions of school desks and chairs, and the exquisitely made high chairs and babies' cradles which have often been handed down through families and are still undergoing the rough and tumble of daily use.

Memories of Childhood will help the would-be-collector to establish the basic know-how needed, firstly, to recognise period style and to understand some of the pitfalls and problems involved in collecting, and secondly, the price guides will give the reader a clear idea of their current market value.

While focusing on those periods from which the reader is most likely to find examples, the book identifies the different categories of childhood antiques. The historical background is given within specific settings such as 'The Victorian Schoolroom', 'The Edwardian Nursery' and 'The 1930s Girl's Room', for example, where a colourful picture is built up showing the kind of artefacts that were in common use at the time. The newcomer to collecting is told exactly what to look for, how to recognize the work of various craftsmen and women, how to avoid fakes and reproductions, and how to check for damage and repairs.

The price guide, featured at the end of each entry, consists of a panel showing a selection of antiques of the type and period under discussion, all captioned and price coded. (See the Price Guide below for the key to the price codes.) Generally, the childhood antiques throughout this volume represent the middle section of the market with the addition of one or two rarer items for greater contrast.

While the current value of childhood collectables can vary enormously from one area to another, you should remember that several factors play a part in determining this such as, the condition and availability of an item, and present day fashion.

By helping you to identify period pieces and to recognize potential antiques from your own childhood, I hope this informative and beautifully illustrated book will give you the expertise to seek out and buy with confidence, and that collecting will always be a great joy and pleasure. I wish you luck in your search.

Tony Curtis

PRICE GUIDE

KEY	❺ £200-£400
❶ £10-£30	❻ £400-£750
❷ £30-£60	❼ £750-£1500
❸ £60-£100	❽ £1500-£6000
❹ £100-£200	❾ £6000 plus

The Regency Nursery

The idea of the nursery came into being in the Regency era, when it was generally a cheerful room crammed with toys and books

With the growing realization that children had special needs and distinct interests, the nursery came into its own as a separate room during the Regency period. It was a colourful, lively place, cheerfully decorated and equipped with child-sized furniture and an abundance of books and toys. It was also noisy and crowded, since children of widely different ages used it, and it had to function simultaneously as playroom and schoolroom, patrolled by nurses and governesses. Here babies were fed and bedded down, infants romped, and boys and girls did their lessons. Regency informality and permissiveness made the nursery a less confining place than it became in Victorian times, and children of both sexes enjoyed a good deal of freedom to behave as they liked in their own domain. For many boys, the nursery must have been a haven compared to the later brutalities of public school.

Kept as a child's domain, the nursery at Brodie Castle in Scotland displays a collection of much-loved toys, rocking horses and furniture.

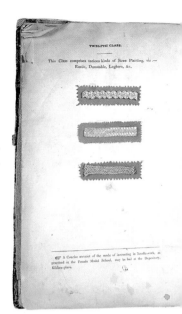

for pure enjoyment rather than instruction and edification. Many parents encouraged their children to behave naturally, and in some instances permissiveness was taken to extraordinary lengths leading to rowdiness and wilful behaviour.

A CHILD'S DOMAIN

These new attitudes promoted the development of the nursery as a separate children's domain. If boisterous play and the scattering of toys and books were now tolerated, there had to be a separate place where they could be done. The social life of adults retained its ceremonious side – especially among the upper classes – and most parents preferred to exclude their offspring (less 'adult' than in earlier times) from such occasions. However charming children might be, there were times when their presence would inevitably be an intrusion.

▲ *A cosy nursery filled with Georgian, Regency and Victorian toys. Since playthings and children's furniture were passed from generation to generation, nurseries often contained a mixture of period styles.*

▶ *This amateur watercolour, which shows nurserymaids playing with their young charges, is a charming evocation of the relaxed and informal atmosphere of many Regency nurseries.*

Before the Regency period, relationships between parents and their offspring, though not necessarily unloving, tended to be formal and remote. Obedience was regarded as the cardinal virtue, and children were expected to behave with the careful gravity of small adults. Then, in the late 18th century, attitudes began to change rapidly as part of a general shift in the values of British society. A new warmth of feeling grew up within the family circle, many formalities were dispensed with (instead of using stiff modes of address, children began to call their parents Mamma and Papa), and there was a new emphasis on companionship. The relaxed and affectionate family portraits painted during the period bear witness to the reality of the change.

The new spirit was reinforced by contemporary ideas about the virtues of naturalness and liberty. These led to an appreciation of childhood as a separate phase of life, and to a belief in the right of children to a wide measure of freedom. Babies were taken out of swaddling clothes, and boys and girls began to be dressed in loose, comfortable outfits that were worn on all but formal occasions. The importance of play was recognized, and children were supplied with many more toys and books that were designed

The Victorian situation, in which parents were simultaneously affectionate and remote, was already anticipated in the 18th century by some aristocrats such as the Duchess of Portland, who saw her son only for 'an hour's jumping' every day. As in Victorian times, too, the nursery was situated at the top of the house, as far away as possible from the main rooms on the ground floor. Nevertheless, the absolute segregation of the children into separate quarters was not typical of the Regency period. Generally speaking, boys and girls had considerable freedom of movement and were allowed a good deal of spare time in which to follow their own inclinations.

A well-equipped nursery made a delightful setting for play, since its furnishings reflected the attention that the child's world was now receiving. Pictorial wallpapers for children could be imported from Germany, designed, for example, to represent the inside of a splendid tent, with the shore and sea glimpsed in the distance through its entrance. The nursery floor might well have been covered with a colourful bordered Brussels carpet, while muslin curtains let in plenty of light.

STURDY FURNITURE

Some of the furniture would have been adult discards or basic but strong units such as deal chests of drawers, but child-sized chairs and other items were commonly found. Though sturdily constructed to withstand rough usage, these followed contemporary styles, even reproducing the delicate detail of their grown-up equivalents. Bamboo chairs, Windsor chairs, chairs with caned seats and other Regency favourites were all produced in miniature for children.

Wooden high chairs had already been known for

▲ *All little girls had to be taught how to sew; this book of needlework instructions contains miniature garments as examples to be copied.*

◀ *Pap boats were used for serving baby food. This splendid example in gold was probably a christening present.*

LIFE AND LEISURE

Children's Dress

UNTIL THE LATE 18TH CENTURY, BOYS AND GIRLS WERE CLAD IN SCALED-DOWN VERSIONS OF ADULT COSTUME, HOWEVER CONFINING AND INAPPROPRIATE THEY HAPPENED TO BE. LITTLE GIRLS WORE STAYS, WHILE BOYS OF EIGHT HAD THEIR HAIR SHORT AND WERE FITTED WITH FASHIONABLE WIGS.

THE FIRST OUTFITS SPECIFICALLY DESIGNED FOR CHILDREN WERE MADE IN THE 1770S, PIONEERING A LOOSER, FREER, MORE 'NATURAL' STYLE THAT SUBSEQUENTLY BECAME THE KEYNOTE OF ADULT FASHION. VERY SMALL CHILDREN CONTINUED TO WEAR DRESSES, IRRESPECTIVE OF SEX, BUT FROM ABOUT THE AGE OF FIVE BOYS WERE EQUIPPED WITH SOFT, FRILLY-COLLARED LAWN OR COTTON SHIRTS, PLAIN OR STRIPED TROUSERS, A SHORT DEEP BLUE JACKET AND A PEAKED CAP. GIRLS WERE EVENTUALLY LIBERATED FROM THEIR UNCOMFORTABLE CORSETS, AND WORE CALF-LENGTH DRESSES WITH BIG SASHES, AND BONNETS OR STRAW HATS.

▲ CHILDREN FROM THE POOREST FAMILIES HAD TO MAKE DO WITH HAND-ME-DOWNS AND RAGS.

▲ THIS LITTLE GIRL IS DRESSED IN THE HEIGHT OF REGENCY FASHION IN A WHITE DRESS AND BLUE SASH.

▲ LOOSE FITTING GARMENTS GAVE REGENCY CHILDREN GREATER FREEDOM FOR ENERGETIC PLAY.

instructional and moralistic works continued to be produced, there were also illustrated books, fairy tale collections, flesh-creeping stories and adventurous yarns that offered nothing more than delight.

YOUTHFUL PLEASURES

One view of life in the Regency nursery is offered by George Cruikshank's engraving of 1826, 'At Home' in the Nursery, or The Masters And Misses Twoshoes' Christmas Party, although allowances must doubtless be made for the exaggerated style of a satirical cartoon. The scene is one of utter chaos. The oldest boy, carrying a small riding crop, waves his hat as he rocks furiously to and fro on a large horse. A nursemaid joggles a baby (still in cap and dress) while three little girls clutching dolls dance

▶ *Pride of place in the nursery was given to the rocking horse.*

◀ *Then, as now, children aped adult behaviour; these children are holding a mock auction.*

▼ *Chaos reigns as naughty children run amok in Cruikshank's engraving 'At Home in the Nursery'.*

some 200 years, and those used in Regency times functioned much as present-day versions do, with a little table which also acted as a restraining bar, and widely splayed legs that ensured stability. Another useful object – often a most elegant and ingeniously crafted piece of work – was the baby-walker, which came in one of two forms, as a push-along trolley or as a broad-based frame that surrounded the infant on all sides.

Miniaturization on an even smaller scale was to be found in the dolls' house and its furniture, which had come into being as an adult fancy but was now relegated to the nursery. The doll herself was an established favourite, whether made of wood, wax or porcelain, and as yet her supremacy was unchallenged by other soft toys. If the parents were rich and doting, the room would be filled with an abundance of other playthings, ranging from the perennial balls, hoops, tops and soldiers to tiny printing presses and an absorbing Regency novelty, the toy theatre.

As in earlier times, parents tried to turn their children's pastimes to educational advantage, but now the pill was usually sweetened, and many toys were made and bought simply for their entertainment value. The same was true of books: although

"AT HOME" in the NURSERY, or The Masters & Misses Twoshoes Christmas Party

around her like the Three Graces. War is being waged against one wall, where two martial figures with trumpet, drums and swords stand on a table or sideboard beneath a Union Jack, fending off two attackers who climb up on chairs to get at them.

On the floor, a girl watches a boy building a house of playing cards, while a muffled coachman drives a coach constructed from a baby's cradle and two chairs, his passengers being two refined dolls with parasols. Toys – rattle, ball, soldiers, horse and cart, and skipping rope – are scattered about everywhere. And to complete this picture of riotous enjoyment, a vast grinning cook or nurse is coming through the door with a big tray of good things for the children to eat.

THE SCHOOLROOM AT HOME

The nursery was also commonly used for more sober purposes, as a schoolroom, and in families where the children had the complete run of the house this might be its primary function. Where it was not the case, there were often young children playing in the room while their elders worked – a situation that cannot have made it easy to study, or to maintain any sort of

reasonable or effective discipline on children.

Permissiveness was least in evidence when it came to spiritual and moral matters. Most parents insisted that their offspring should receive a thorough religious education – and were equally insistent that their daughters should learn graces and accomplishments, such as needlework and musical skills, that would make them attractive prospects for future husbands. Deportment was of particular importance, and both boys and girls were encouraged to acquire an upright posture by a variety of devices including the Astley-Cooper corrective chair, an uncomfortable-looking straight-backed seat which became a feature of nurseries for several generations.

When they reached the age of ten, boys left the nursery for boarding school; most girls remained at home, closer to the life of the nursery, while the governess worked to turn them into young ladies. Although the basic pattern laid down during the Regency period did not change, the 'golden age' soon came to an end with the triumph of Victorian values, which made sure that children were more rigorously disciplined, tightly dressed and segregated from the adults behind the nursery walls.

▲ *An uncomfortable-looking child's correction chair designed to promote an upright posture.*

| LIFE AND LEISURE |

A Regency Education

DESPITE THE AIRING OF SOME PROGRESSIVE IDEAS, THE EDUCATION OF UPPER-CLASS CHILDREN PERPETUATED THE TRADITIONAL DISCRIMINATION BETWEEN THE SEXES. EDUCATION WAS BASED ON THE ASSUMPTION THAT MALES WERE DESTINED FOR THE WORLD OUTSIDE, AND FEMALES FOR THE HOME.

HOWEVER, ALL CHILDREN SPENT THEIR FIRST TEN YEARS AT HOME UNDER THE CARE OF NURSES AND GOVERNESS. THEN, AT TEN, MOST BOYS WENT TO A PUBLIC SCHOOL. DURING THE REGENCY PERIOD MANY OF THESE WERE TERRIFYING, VIOLENT PLACES WHERE GREEK AND LATIN WERE BEATEN INTO THE PUPILS AND THE FAGGING SYSTEM PROMOTED ORGIES OF SADISTIC BULLYING. REFORM WAS ONLY A FEW YEARS AWAY. BUT IN THE MEANTIME SOME PARENTS PREFERRED TO HAVE THEIR BOYS TAUGHT AT HOME BY A TUTOR, BEFORE SENDING THEM DIRECTLY TO OXFORD OF CAMBRIDGE. BY CONTRAST, THE GIRLS WERE TAUGHT 'ACCOMPLISHMENTS' SUCH AS DRAWING, SINGING AND SEWING, BY A GOVERNESS, WHO WAS ALL TOO OFTEN A DISTRESSED GENTLEWOMAN OF NO GREAT EDUCATIONAL ATTAINMENT.

▲ A SCHOOLROOM AT HARROW IN 1816. SEVERAL CLASSES ARE BEING TAUGHT AND DISCIPLINE IS STRICT.

▶ COPYING AND LEARNING BY ROTE DID NOT ALWAYS INSPIRE ENTHUSIASM IN YOUNG SCHOLARS.

▶▶ DESPITE THE SPREAD OF LIBERAL ATTITUDES, SOME SCHOOLMASTERS CONTINUED TO BELIEVE IN FLOGGING.

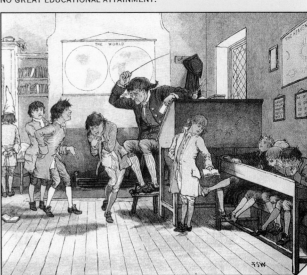

Dolls' Houses

Georgian and Regency dolls' houses and their miniature furniture
provide many fascinating insights into the way fashions and people's
lives have changed over the last three centuries

The earliest English dolls' houses, dating from the first half of the 18th century, tell us more of how the adults of the times lived than of how their children amused themselves. In some respects this is a pity, but most surviving 18th-century dolls' houses or 'baby houses' as they were known (dolls were referred to as 'babies' until the beginning of the 19th century) are such splendid constructions fitted with such beautiful and precious furniture, that it is impossible to imagine small children playing unsupervised with their fragile contents.

Dolls' houses are a collector's and a social historian's delight. Rooms and details of contemporary life, of which little or no trace remains in grand Georgian houses, are preserved in miniature in the baby houses of the period.

The fact that children have always enjoyed playing with dolls and miniature models of everyday household objects is evident from finds at Egyptian, Greek and Roman archaeological sites. There are accounts of Greek and Roman children constructing houses, and some of the ancient toy chairs, stools, pots and dishes have survived, the best preserved miniatures being those made of lead.

There are also records of German dolls' houses built as early as the 16th century,

▶ *Because Georgian dolls' houses are now so rare, an alternative is a reproduction house in the Georgian style, such as this lovely example.*

although the earliest surviving example is dated 1611. Most were commissioned by rich noblemen for themselves or as magnificent gifts, although some were apparently assembled as cabinets of curiosities and exhibited to the public, who paid to see them at fairs. It was the work of these highly skilled German workers that led to the popularity of the dolls' house spreading to the rest of Europe.

None of the early German houses seem to have been made as a child's toy; many were

Nostell Priory Dolls' House

PERHAPS THE MOST BEAUTIFUL OF ENGLISH DOLLS' HOUSES, THE
NOSTELL PRIORY HOUSE WAS BUILT CIRCA 1735 AND IS THOUGHT
TO BE A REPLICA OF THE DESIGN OF NOSTELL ITSELF. THE
ELABORATE FACADE SLIDES ACROSS TO REVEAL THE NINE ROOMS,
WHOSE INTERIORS ARE STILL IN THEIR ORIGINAL STATE.

simply far too high for a child to reach. However, smaller, less impressively furnished houses have survived from later in the 17th century, as well as individual rooms, usually kitchens, which may well have served for a child's play, or more likely, instruction in the skills of housekeeping.

CABINET HOUSES

These splendid German creations with their magnificent wax-headed dolls engaged in every possible domestic pursuit appealed to wealthy Dutch merchants and their families, who took to decorating and furnishing houses even more impressively than their German counterparts. Most Dutch 'cabinet houses' were in fact cabinets, beautiful pieces of furniture with locking doors which opened to reveal a series of lavishly appointed rooms.

In style, the two best-known English baby houses of the early 18th century owe much to the Dutch houses. They were both

◀ Dolls' houses were at one time considered too precious for children to play with, and were kept well out of reach on tall cabinets. Although they are still highly prized, the most appropriate place to display a dolls' house is in the nursery – as long as children appreciate its fragility.

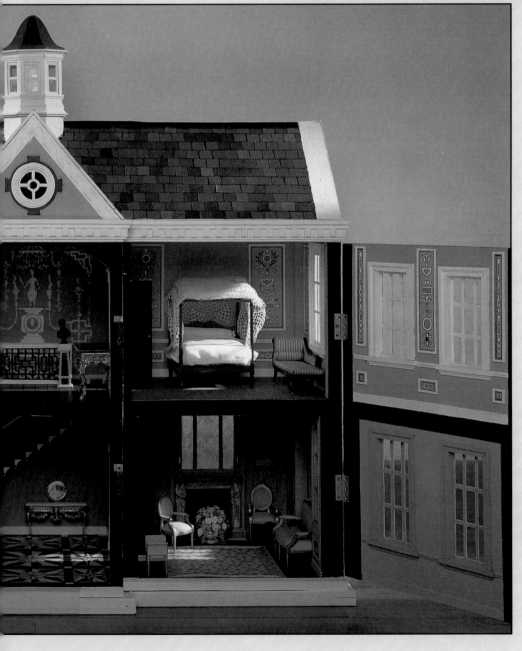

part of the furniture of stately homes, one at Nostell Priory in Yorkshire, the other at Uppark in Sussex, where they have been lovingly preserved and are still on show. It is not known in which room of the house they were originally displayed; their dolls and dolls' house furniture are not of such high quality as is found in the best Dutch houses, but they were certainly too delicate and fine for the nursery.

In the Nostell Priory house, the Palladian facade is in two halves, which slide apart to reveal the nine-room interior. The Uppark house has a better arrangement for access to its nine rooms, each being fitted with a hinged front. The panelling and mouldings round the windows on the inside of each of these doors match the other three walls of the rooms perfectly.

MINIATURE FURNITURE

The furniture in these two famous baby houses includes many beautifully crafted chairs and tables, miniature paintings, marble chimneypieces, silver firebacks and candle sconces, even mahogany doors with tiny brass locks, clearly pieces made specially when the houses were built.

There are slightly incongruous additions in the houses, like the alabaster tea-table with teapot, bowls and saucers made of the same material in the housekeeper's room at Uppark. Similar alabaster sets have turned up in other English and continental houses of the period and were clearly sold by toymakers as standard dolls' house equipment.

The Georgian dolls' houses which have survived intact were for the most part well looked after, as they were important family treasures. Obviously children did play with dolls' houses during the period, although unfortunately there are no contemporary accounts of how they did so.

Town Houses

In the first half of the 19th century, dolls' houses varied enormously in size, solidity and the quality of their carpentry. Wide-fronted town houses with magnificently detailed architectural facades were still produced in imitation of 18th-century baby houses, but they were clearly intended to be played with by children, rather than shown to admiring guests. In many cases, the name of the houses is written over the front door, often accompanied by the date the house was presented to its young owner.

The dolls which lived in English dolls' houses were usually jointed wooden ones of German origin, of the type known as Grödnertals, after the area which specialized in their production. Much of the best furniture was also of German origin, but English toy-makers, in Birmingham and London especially, produced an enor-mous variety of miniature objects in wood, tin, copper and pewter. Spare metal could be cast in crudely-made moulds to make anything from a dining-room table to a teaspoon. The best quality pewter, Britannia metal, with a high tin content, could make a row of dishes on a pine dresser gleam like silver, but the cheaper varieties with more lead, would bend out of shape in no time at all. Wooden pieces were often finely carved.

◀ *A painted wooden dolls' house (c. 1840) consisting of three storeys, known as 'The Dublin Townhouse'. The bottom two rooms are furnished more basically than those of the upper two floors, as was the case in real life. In the kitchen is a range and an assortment of pots and pans.*

PRICE GUIDE **8**

PRICE GUIDE

◀▼ Known as 'The Town Dolls' House', this house is on display at the Bethnal Green Museum, London. Built between 1840 and 1850 in the form of a substantial family house, the facade is painted in a stone yellow which is typical of many mid 19th-century houses built in south London. The fine craftsmanship is evident on the carved wooden front door and on the elegant balustrades on the balcony. The ten rooms inside are furnished in a variety of styles, although the quality is not as good as that of the exterior. Although the bedroom is furnished with a fitted carpet, as are many of the rooms, such luxury was quite rare in reality. All the main rooms have fireplaces and central lights hanging from the ceiling. Because it is a museum piece, this house does not carry a price guide.

▲▶ With its four floors and stylish Georgian frontage, 'The Town Dolls' House' is built on a larger scale than 'The Dublin Townhouse' (left) and reflects the greater opulence of its owners. The main entertaining room on the first floor is spacious and boasts gilded cornices, a ceiling rosette with a hanging glass chandelier, a marble-topped pedestal table, a marquetry side table, plush velvet upholstery on the sofa and chairs and many other fine features. The framed portraits on the walls are possibly of the actual family and the glass-encased clock, wine decanters, goblets and fluted glass candlesticks that adorn the room may well be scaled down versions of the real ones owned by the family.

PRICE GUIDE

Villas and Shops

The manufacture of dolls' houses in Regency and early Victorian times was still very much in the hands of individual craftsmen. There was no organized industry in Britain until much later in the 19th century, when firms like Lines Brothers, who subsequently became Triang, started to produce a range of standard models. As the demand for dolls' houses grew, more and more short cuts were taken by manufacturers in their decoration: sheets of specially printed paper would be stuck on to represent the brickwork or stonework of the facade.

Most Victorian dolls' houses are modest dwellings compared to their 18th-century predecessors. Many were made to represent middle-class, suburban vil-las and even two-roomed country cottages. The front usually opened in two hinged sections, but in smaller houses the whole front might be a door. Stylized central staircases, placed peri-lously close to the front door, became a more or less standard feature. Wallpapers were improvised out of all kinds of scraps of paper and material, while curtains, bed-hangings, quilts and upholstery were likely to be the work of the young mistress or of members of the family.

As well as dolls' houses, there have survived a few Georgian and Victorian examples of individual rooms or shops fitted out with an intriguing display of miniature wares, reminiscent of the educational kitchens made in 17th-century Germany.

▲ Known as the Regency Villa, this finely modelled house of painted wood was manufactured in 1889. The porticoed front door opens and the roof and balcony are covered with delicately patterned tiles. The back opens to reveal the interior, consisting of four rooms and a stairwell. To the right are the stables, with an enclosed yard, kennel, hayloft and bell tower. To the left is the conservatory, which is filled with assorted potted plants in china pots.

PRICE GUIDE **8**

◀ As well as dolls' houses, shops and market stalls were also constructed. This children's bazaar, now in Bethnal Green Museum, London, was made in England circa 1830, with a mixture of English and German components. It is indeed a miniature and measures only 12 inches (30 cm) high. Because it is a museum piece, it does not carry a price guide.

PRICE GUIDE

▲▼ 'The Long House' was made circa 1870,
and is based on a traditional late Victorian
suburban home. The standard of carpentry is
very high, and although most of the rooms have
been re-papered and re-carpeted the period feel is
undisturbed. Because the house belongs to the
National Trust, it does not carry a price guide.

PRICE GUIDE

Genuine Regency dolls' houses are beyond the scope of all but the wealthiest collectors, and if and when they do turn up at auction they fetch extremely high prices. Such early dolls' houses can, however, be seen at museums.

A finely made house, dating from around 1805, is on view in the Southwold Museum in Suffolk; another is the large dolls' house exhibited at Audley End in Essex. A visit to the Bethnal Green Museum of Childhood, which has a large collection of dolls'

houses, is also helpful. Here, for example, the visitor can see the exquisite Tate Baby House, one of the finest 18th-century houses, noted for its intricate carpentry and attention to architectural detail. Many Regency houses retain 18th-century characteristics, particularly in the design of fireplaces and spit racks, and the collector is well advised to acquire familiarity with the period in order to know what features to look for. Viewing these splendid dolls' houses also gives the enthusiast an idea of how to furnish the Regency-style dolls' houses produced from mid-Victorian times to the present day.

REPRODUCTION DOLLS' HOUSES
Finding 19th-century dolls' houses that are in good condition or worth restoring is very difficult and collectors are now turning to models commercially produced in the 1920s and 1930s by firms like the Lines Brothers who traded under the name of Triang (and continued to produce dolls' houses until the 1950s). These now have some 'antique' value themselves and many are not only copies of genuine buildings but extremely well made.

The best place to look for these repro-

Architectural Styles

GEORGIAN AND REGENCY DOLLS' HOUSES COPIED THE ARCHITECTURAL STYLES OF ACTUAL HOUSES OF THE PERIOD. THE HOUSE ON THE LEFT WAS CONSTRUCTED CIRCA 1810-1820 AND IS AN EXACT REPLICA OF THE GATEHOUSE AT WAYNEFLEETE, A GOTHIC CASTLE. THE HOUSE ON THE RIGHT IS KNOWN AS 'THE GREAT HOUSE' AND WAS MADE AROUND 1750.

The Blackett Baby House

THE BLACKETT BABY HOUSE WAS NAMED AFTER THE LADY WHO DONATED IT TO THE MUSEUM OF LONDON, WHERE IT IS NOW HOUSED. IT WAS MADE IN THE MID-18TH CENTURY AND IS PERFECTLY SCALED FOR A YOUNG CHILD TO PLAY WITH. THE CRAFTSMANSHIP IS FINELY DETAILED THROUGHOUT, WITH AN IMPRESSIVELY CARVED FACADE AND BEAUTIFULLY DECORATED ROOMS. THE STAND, HOWEVER, IS NOT AS WELL MADE.

EXCLUDING THE KITCHEN, THE THREE MAIN ROOMS: DRAWING ROOM, BEDROOM AND DINING ROOM, ALL HAVE CORNICES, SKIRTING BOARDS AND CHAIR RAILS, FITTING WITH THE PERIOD. THE GILDED MOULDING, ADDED AT A LATER DATE, DOES NOT REALLY BLEND WITH THE OTHERWISE AUTHENTIC 18TH-CENTURY DECOR. THE HAND-PAINTED WALLPAPER IS DIFFICULT TO DATE, BUT THE BLUE CHINTZ IN THE DRAWING ROOM IS OF THE TYPE TO BE FOUND IN A GEORGIAN HOUSE. MUCH OF THE FURNITURE, INCLUDING THE BED, IS ORIGINAL.

① THE FANLIGHT OVER THE DOOR IS ONE OF THE FINEST EVER FOUND ON A MINIATURE HOUSE.

② THE SASH WINDOWS ACTUALLY OPEN.

③ ORIGINAL 18TH-CENTURY WAX DOLLS IN CONTEMPORARY COSTUME WORN BY THE MIDDLE CLASSES.

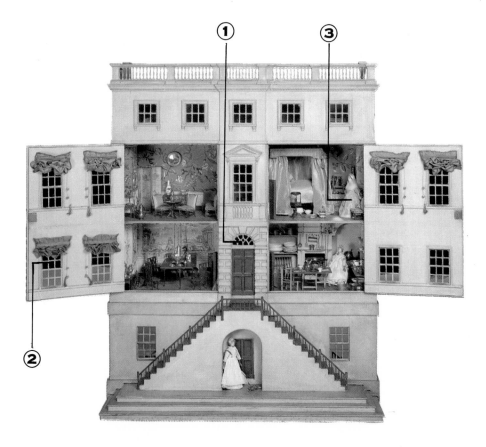

·CLOSE UP·

① STAIR RUNNER

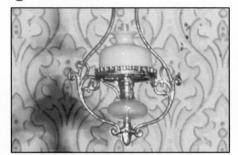

② HANGING LIGHT

③ GEORGIAN DOLL

④ BALCONY RAIL

⑤ CHINA COFFEE SERVICE

⑥ MINIATURE FURNITURE

① ALONG THE CENTRE OF THE STAIRCASE IS AN ACTUAL CARPET CAREFULLY WOVEN WITH A SCALED-DOWN PATTERN.

② SOME ROOMS HAD DETAILED FITTINGS SUCH AS HANGING LIGHTS IN ALL THE MAIN ROOMS.

③ MANY GEORGIAN DOLLS' HOUSES COME COMPLETE WITH A SET OF DOLLS MADE OF WOOD OR WAX.

④ THE WOODEN BALUSTER RAIL SHOWS THE FINE WORKMANSHIP OF A HIGHLY SKILLED CRAFTSMAN.

⑤ MINIATURE CHINA COFFEE SERVICE MADE TO SCALE IN A DELICATE BLUE AND WHITE PATTERN WITH ROSES.

⑥ MINIATURE WOODEN PEDESTAL TABLE AND MATCHING STOOL QUITE PRIMITIVELY CARVED.

duction dolls' houses is at the regular dolls, dolls' houses and miniatures fairs which take place all over Britain. Even so, such pieces are not cheap and can cost in excess of £500-£700, with examples dating from Edwardian times costing even more. The major auction houses in Britain hold regular sales of dolls' houses and dolls' house furniture and utensils, and the novice collector is well advised to study the catalogues and if possible attend one or two sales. This is a great help in increasing knowledge about what is available and what it costs.

MODERN COPIES

Making and furnishing period dolls' houses is a popular hobby not only in Britain but also abroad, particularly in the US. Since there is such a shortage of genuine antique dolls' houses, many collectors are turning to these models and using them as a starting point for collecting old miniature furniture. This seems a very sensible compromise. Old dolls' houses are relatively scarce, but miniature furniture seems to be more readily available in auctions and antique fairs.

Much miniature furniture is difficult to date since Regency-style furniture was made for Victorian dolls' houses, just as it is made for modern ones. Victorian dolls'

kitchens, for example, often had 18th-century spits and ranges, because they were more picturesque than contemporary ones. Similarly, late Victorian bedrooms continued to be filled with enormous four-poster beds. The date of pieces should not worry the amateur collector too much. Correct period style and quality craftmanship are arguably more important in this field.

DO-IT-YOURSELF

Period dolls' houses are now available in kit form or fully made up and a wide range of miniature furniture is also available. Enthusiasts can therefore create and furnish their own Regency-style dolls' house using colour schemes and papers that fit the period, and modern paint techniques to give the desired antique effect to furniture. There are specialist magazines and books that offer advice and information of all aspects of dolls' house model-making and miniature furniture, and the popularity of this hobby shows how satisfying it is.

POINTS TO WATCH

■ Genuine Regency dolls' houses are rare and expensive; reproductions of the style are common. If you do buy a modern reproduction, make sure the architectural features are

all technically correct for the Regency period.
■ Miniature furniture and accessories are difficult to date; better a faithful modern reproduction than a suspect antique.
■ Antique dolls' houses are often fragile: seek professional advice before attempting detailed restoration.

▼ *Although the front of this object looks like a dolls' house, it is in fact a child's wardrobe, designed to look like a country mansion.*

Cots, Cribs and Cradles

By the Regency period a variety of cots and cradles had been developed to lull babies to sleep or to show them off as their parents' pride and joy

In Europe the traditional method of lulling a baby to sleep has long been by rocking it in a cradle or swinging cot. In Roman Britain, cradles of hammock form were evidently slung between the branches of trees and even before that time simple rocking cradles were made by hollowing out tree trunks.

By the Middle Ages, though, cradles had become quite sophisticated and were often decorated with elaborate carving and panelling. Although no medieval examples have survived, contemporary illustrations and written accounts show that they obviously provided the prototypes for the 17th- and 18th-century cradles with which we are familiar today.

The terminology surrounding cots and cradles is confused. In general, the word 'cradle' describes either the type mounted at floor level on two curved wooden rockers or that suspended between two wooden uprights joined by stretchers. The term 'cot' or 'crib' implies the immovable, high-sided baby's bed supported on four straight legs which was devised around 1800 for children of toddler age, but which today is used for new-born babies too. In both the 18th and 19th centuries, though, the term 'cot' often distinguished the swing type of cradle from its rocking counterpart.

WICKER WORK

During the 17th and 18th centuries the appearance of cradles was quite varied. Probably the most common type – although no English examples have survived – was made from wicker. In effect large baskets with one end extending upwards to form a hood, wicker cradles, mounted on wooden rockers, appear to have been used in households at all social levels. Royal or noble babies also had a very grand 'cradle of estate' in which they were proudly displayed to admiring visitors. If the baby had only one cradle, its status could be raised for such occasions by temporarily draping the hood with a costly textile. The interior of the hood was sometimes lined with fabric to protect the baby from draughts.

Rocking cradles of all types were generally kept in motion by placing a foot on one of the rockers, a practice which left the hands free for more industrious occupations, but wicker ones sometimes had special rocking handles woven into their sides.

Large numbers of 17th-century wicker cradles have survived in America, where

they are popularly believed to have arrived with the Pilgrim Fathers, hence their common name 'Mayflower cradles'. They were especially popular, too, in Holland, where they were sometimes accompanied by a *bakermat,* a floor-level seat with a slightly raised back support which was used by the wet-nurse or mother while changing and feeding the baby.

▲ *The infant King of Rome, only son of Napoleon Bonaparte, with his mother, Arch-Duchess Marie-Louise. The boy-king had several magnificent cradles of estate.*

The largest number of surviving 17th- and early 18th-century cradles are of wooden panelled construction. Oak was the most common choice of timber, but elm, beech and other indigenous woods were also used. Until the end of the 16th century it was common for the head-end of the cradle simply to have raised sides, but after 1600 a full hood became more normal.

PLAIN AND FANCY

The humblest cradles – made for country cottages and farmhouses – usually had completely plain or chip-carved panels, but more costly versions had elaborate carved designs and, occasionally, wood inlay of contrasting colours. Traces of colour on some examples indicate that, like so much early woodwork, they were additionally painted and gilded. Early 18th-century cradles often had fielded panels.

The corners of the cradle generally had turned finials which were used to rock it back and forth. Sometimes these were present only at one end, sometimes on both ends and on the front of the hood as well. The hood itself was occasionally hinged to allow easy access to the baby and a small storage cupboard was often present at its back. Some cradles had holes or metal loops along their sides through which ropes or leather thongs were passed to hold the baby in place. The bottom of the cradle frequently had similar holes for the interlaced ropes which supported the bedding – a feature of contemporary beds – but sometimes the base was of solid wood or constructed of horizontal laths.

The rockers were usually cut into the ends of the cradle, or attached via short turned supports. In both cases, they often displayed some degree of ornamental shaping. The hood, too, showed variation in

shape. During the 17th century hoods were mostly flat-topped and in the early 18th they were often of ogee arch form.

A good number of surviving oak cradles are carved with initials and a date. These usually indicate the birthday and name of the cradle's first occupant, but sometimes refer to the reigning monarch. They should not always be relied on as a method of dating as cradles were often passed down through several generations of a family and may well have been inscribed at a later date. Victorian reproductions were also made, often of pine painted and grained to simulate oak.

▲ *Victorian and Edwardian cots are just as practical as modern ones – themselves often copies of old designs. This swinging cot in turned wood is draped in 19th-century style.*

Pine was also used in earlier times for those cradles of estate which were completely upholstered in silk or velvet, trimmed with gold and silver fringes and tassels and finished with gilt-headed nails. Traditionally, they were placed beneath a matching canopy, and were used entirely as a symbol of status and wealth. During the 18th century this practice gradually diminished in importance except among the royal family.

▶ *This late 17th-century rocking cradle from Germany became part of the Royal Collection in 1843. Resplendently carved and gilded, it was originally made for a wealthy or aristocratic family.*

◀ *A swinging cot made for the Princess Royal in 1843 and subsequently used by all Victoria's children. It is made of mahogany, with brass mounts. The silk hangings are not original.*

Late Regency Cot

THIS MAGNIFICENT MAHOGANY COT CARRIES A BRASS TRADE PLATE ATTRIBUTING IT TO THE FIRM OF MORGAN SANDERS, WHO SPECIALIZED IN PATENT AND CONVERTIBLE FURNITURE. THIS COT, MADE AROUND THE 1820S, CAN READILY BE DISMANTLED FOR EASE OF TRANSPORT AND WAS PRESUMABLY INTENDED FOR THE CHILDREN OF A FAMILY IN THE COLONIAL SERVICE. TWO SMALL CHILDREN COULD FIT IN IT COMFORTABLY.

ALL THE WOODWORK, INCLUDING THE SLATS IN THE BASE, IS MAHOGANY, AND ALL THE METAL-WORK — CASTORS, HINGES, CORNER-PIECES, PINS, FITTINGS AND FINIALS — IS BRASS. THE CANEWORK PANELS DROP INTO PLACE AND SWIVEL ON BRASS LUGS SET INTO THE BASE FRAME. EACH DOUBLE PANEL IS HINGED IN THE CENTRE. THE DRAPED AND SWAGGED CANOPY MAY ONCE HAVE BEEN COVERED WITH MOSQUITO NETTING.

① CANOPY FOR MOSQUITO NETTING

② BRASS CASTORS AND FITTINGS

③ SLATTED BASE

④ CANEWORK PANELS

Doll's Cradle

THIS CHARMING SWINGING CRADLE WAS MADE OF POLISHED STEEL TOWARD THE END OF THE 19TH CENTURY. TOO SMALL FOR A BABY, IT WAS INTENDED FOR A DOLL. THE CURVED END-PIECE IS FOR A DRAPE.

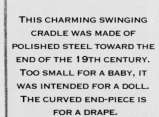

Until roughly 1750, cradles of swing type appear to have been rare in Britain, although quite common on the Continent. The earliest known English example was reputedly made for Henry V (although it is actually late 15th century) and after that they appeared intermittently as cradles of estate.

Their increase in popularity coincided with the widespread use of mahogany for furniture. Mahogany, a hard, dense wood ideally suited to fine carving and cabinet work, was seldom used for cradles of rocker type. Even in oak, rocking cradles soon became unfashionable in the latter half of the 18th century.

Although a number of mahogany swinging cradles were made with solid panelled sides, the majority of 18th-century examples had a rectangular framework containing large panels of woven split cane and an arched hood constructed in the same way. Sometimes the framework of the hood was covered with fabric instead. By the end of the century, rows of turned spindles had begun to provide an alternative to split cane sides and the hood was usually dispensed with.

The use of open-sided cradles is generally attributed to a concern for hygiene, as the freer circulation of air would have been much healthier for the

baby. It has been suggested that split cane cradles were relatively cheap to make and therefore were less of a loss if they had to be destroyed after an infectious illness, but the real reason was probably just fashion.

The uprights and the stretcher (or stretchers) joining them varied in complexity from simple turnings around the middle of the century to more elaborate foliate carving in the 1760s and 1770s and classical columns mounted on splayed and reeded legs toward 1800.

The Regency period saw great variety in cradle design. For the average home, simple cradles with cane panels continued to be made, either in

▼ AN 1870S VERSION OF A GOTHIC CRADLE. THE MAHOGANY FRAME IS FILLED WITH CANEWORK AND THE HOOD COVERED WITH GREEN VELVET. THE INTERIOR IS PADDED.

PRICE GUIDE 6

▼ THIS FRENCH CRADLE DATES FROM THE 1860S. THE FRET-WORK FRAME, ROCKERS AND SLATS ARE OF FRUIT WOOD, WHILE THE SPINDLES IN THE SIDES ARE BRASS.

PRICE GUIDE 7

▲ A FRENCH CRIB OF AROUND 1900. THE TURNED WILLOW FRAME AND WICKER INFILL HAVE BEEN PAINTED BLUE.

PRICE GUIDE 5

▼ THIS NARROW WICKER CRIB OF THE 1880S MAY HAVE BEEN FOR A DOLL OR A VERY YOUNG BABY.

PRICE GUIDE 5

▲ THIS IMPOSING FOUR-SQUARE CRADLE IS IN THE EUROPEAN BIEDEMEIER STYLE. MADE OF WALNUT, IT DATES FROM THE 1830S.

PRICE GUIDE 7

▲ A COLLAPSIBLE FRENCH COT OF THE LATE 19TH CENTURY MADE ENTIRELY FROM WHITE-PAINTED CAST IRON.

PRICE GUIDE 5

mahogany or rosewood, although open-sided mahogany cradles with turned spindles became more popular.

For the wealthy, some extraordinarily elaborate cots were devised, particularly for royal babies for whom cradles of estate were still used. The young George IV, for example was publicly displayed in a gilt cradle under a canopy of crimson velvet. Many were designed in full classical style incorporating Greek and Roman motifs and a great deal of gilding. Elaborate drapery – a feature given great prominence in interior design generally – played an important role in their design. Curtains forming a hood

were either hung from a circular canopy or were loosely draped over a metal bar forming an extension of one upright.

Not every cradle had a rocking facility although Sheraton in his *Cabinet Dictionary* of 1803 illustrated a 'swinging Crib Bed' with a clock-spring device invented by a Mr. Holinshade of Drury Lane which could keep the cot moving for up to 20 minutes.

Other designers devised elaborate cots in fashionable Regency styles. George Smith, for example, showed swing-cots in rather heavy Gothic style. For older babies, the Regency period saw an increase in the number of modern-style cribs,

with a rectangular box composed of turned uprights mounted on four straight legs. In 1776 the joiner Catherine Naish had supplied George III with both a split cane cradle and a 'couch Bedstead on castors' with 'mahogany Laths and Pillars' and 'turned Bannisters to keep the Prince from falling out'. This presumably was the forerunner of the modern-day immovable cot or crib.

The rapid increase in popularity of this type of cot during the 19th century can be attributed to the growing custom of leaving the baby in the nursery at night rather than alongside its mother's bed, within the confines of the bed hangings.

POINTS TO WATCH
■ Georgian cots were narrower than is usual today, owing to the custom of swaddling babies still prevalent in many households.

■ Many oak antiques were carved with spurious dates and extra decoration by the Victorians. Victorian work can easily be recognized as it is shallow and machine-cut, showing no chisel-marks, and lacks the vigour of earlier carving.

■ Check the uprights and metal fittings of swinging cots; they were subject to wear and may have been replaced.

■ Some cots and cradles are marriages of two pieces. Check for different-coloured woods.

The Rattle

The rattle is the most basic and enduring of objects made for small babies. Georgian and Regency rattles are often masterpieces of craftsmanship, as much family heirlooms as toys

One characteristic of late Georgian and Regency times was a caring, libertarian attitude towards children; this extended to the very young. A symptom of this was that the centuries-old custom of swaddling – binding up babies so closely in swaddling clothes that they could not move their limbs – was finally abandoned. Much of the child-care advice given by the leading Regency authority, William Buchan, sounds very modern. He denounced 'stays and bandages', the convenient custom of putting children to sleep or pacifying them with drugs or sweetened foods, and the practice of sending boys away to school at too tender an age. Buchan even pointed out the health hazards of early employment – with less effect, however, since that only affected the children of the poor.

THE WET NURSE
Buchan and other writers also proclaimed the virtues of breast-feeding. Until this time, upper-class mothers had employed a wet nurse – that is, a nursing mother who would feed her employer's child as well as – or instead of – her own. Wet nurses had a rather unsavoury reputation, and doubts about them were reinforced by the widespread belief that the nurse transmitted elements of her character to the baby through her milk! As a result, in the 1780s some great ladies, led by the Duchess of Devonshire,

◀ *Rattles have entranced babies and young children alike for centuries. Early examples were made from bronze or terracotta, often shaped as animals. Roman rattles featured small bells, while in the 17th century, as well as simple wooden rattles, combinations of rattle, coral teething stick, whistle and bells were made in gold and silver. These remained popular in the 18th and 19th centuries.*

actually began to breast-feed their own children.

There were a number of positive reasons for employing a wet nurse, including the mother's rapid recovery of a desirably fashionable figure and her ability to socialize to the full, and the practice did not completely disappear until late in the 19th century. Where either the mother or the baby was incapable of breast-feeding, the alternative was the feeding bottle. Delightful examples in transfer-printed earthenware have survived from the Regency period, along with papboats – which were filled with mushy cereal mixtures – for slightly older infants. However, these elegant objects were not very effective in sustaining life and warding off disease – as was still the case when Charles Dickens came to write his novel *Great Expectations*, in which Mrs Gargery is always willing to boast that the hero, young Pip, was successfully 'raised by hand'.

A BABY'S FIRST TOY

Freed from swaddling clothes, the baby became a more active and assertive being, and therefore a more attractive one. He, or she, was certainly now more likely to receive attention and to be played with. But, given the baby's helplessness and lack of mobility, there was no new toy that even the most devoted parent could devise which compared with the age-old favourite:

'Behold the child, by Nature's kindly law,
Pleased with a rattle, tickled with a straw.'

So wrote the 18th-century poet Alexander Pope, neatly summarizing the simple pleasure offered by a rattle. This was the baby's first toy, one which entertained when nothing else could, whether manipulated by mother or nurse, or pushed, shaken and thrown when the infant had learned to grasp at objects. It occupied the attention, the mysterious noises from its interior and the jingling of its attached bells tickling the fancy even before the baby had developed enough sense of rhythm to use it as a musical instrument.

CHRISTENING PRESENTS

Although it could be made of precious metal and intricately designed, the rattle was fundamentally a simple device. A gourd with some dried peas inside it, or a pot containing a pebble, might entrance a baby as completely as the finest example of the craftsman's skill. So it is not surprising that rattles have been found all over the world, and seem to date back to the dawn of human history. The decorative impulse – or perhaps the shrewd insight that baby would be all the better for something interesting to look at – found expression early on, notably in the terracotta rattles fashioned by the Romans in various animal shapes. But technically there was no significant development until the 17th century, when combinations of rattle, coral teething stick, whistle and bells were made. These were often exquisite and expensive objects, to judge from the £1.10s paid by the Earl of Bristol for 'a corrail [coral] set in gold', and often originated as christening presents. The custom carried on into the 18th and 19th centuries: the Prince Regent used a splendid gold rattle, made in 1760, which was decorated in the rococo style, and Queen Victoria passed on to her descendants a Regency rattle that had been made in 1806.

THE GENERATION GAME

It was indeed characteristic of such deluxe, hallmarked objects that they should have been handed down from generation to generation. Many of them have survived in excellent condition down to the present day, and this fact suggests that they were not left for long periods of time in the clutches of vigorously growing infants, but were only used by, or under the eye of, the nurse or mother; a ribbon, strung through the little ring commonly found on this type of rattle, attached it securely to the woman's girdle or belt.

Even in Georgian and Regency times, many rattles must have been home-made objects that cost

▲ *Rattles with a coral teething stick or ivory ring served the dual purpose of both keeping the baby amused and giving it something to cut its teeth on. Coral was often chosen, not only because the colour was so pleasing, but also because it was reputed to cool the baby's sore gums. Some people even believed that coral would protect the child and keep it safe from evil spirits.*

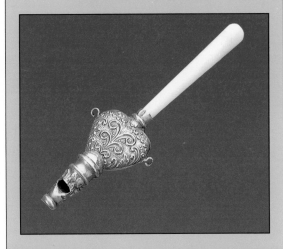

AN ATTRACTIVE, LATE REGENCY HEART-SHAPED RATTLE IN SILVER WITH A PRETTY MOTHER-OF-PEARL HANDLE. THE RATTLE INCORPORATES A SIMPLE WHISTLE.

AN IVORY TEETHING RING WITH A SILVER SHELL-SHAPED RATTLE ATTACHED. THIS SERVED THE DUAL PURPOSE OF ENTERTAINING THE CHILD AND SOOTHING IT.

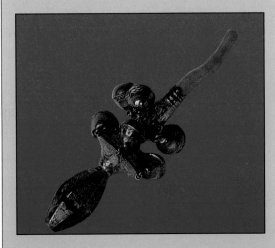

AN INTRICATELY-WORKED RATTLE WITH A WHISTLE, BELLS AND A CORAL TEETHING STICK. THESE WERE OFTEN GIVEN AS CHRISTENING PRESENTS IN REGENCY AND VICTORIAN TIMES.

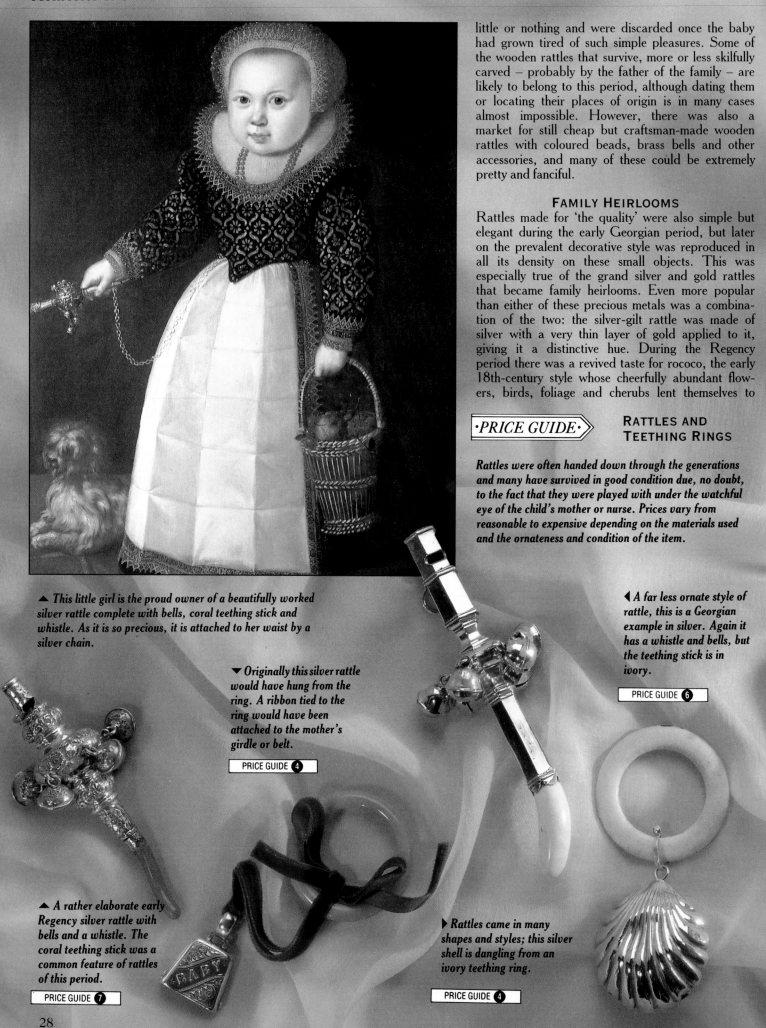

little or nothing and were discarded once the baby had grown tired of such simple pleasures. Some of the wooden rattles that survive, more or less skilfully carved – probably by the father of the family – are likely to belong to this period, although dating them or locating their places of origin is in many cases almost impossible. However, there was also a market for still cheap but craftsman-made wooden rattles with coloured beads, brass bells and other accessories, and many of these could be extremely pretty and fanciful.

FAMILY HEIRLOOMS

Rattles made for 'the quality' were also simple but elegant during the early Georgian period, but later on the prevalent decorative style was reproduced in all its density on these small objects. This was especially true of the grand silver and gold rattles that became family heirlooms. Even more popular than either of these precious metals was a combination of the two: the silver-gilt rattle was made of silver with a very thin layer of gold applied to it, giving it a distinctive hue. During the Regency period there was a revived taste for rococo, the early 18th-century style whose cheerfully abundant flowers, birds, foliage and cherubs lent themselves to

·PRICE GUIDE· RATTLES AND TEETHING RINGS

Rattles were often handed down through the generations and many have survived in good condition due, no doubt, to the fact that they were played with under the watchful eye of the child's mother or nurse. Prices vary from reasonable to expensive depending on the materials used and the ornateness and condition of the item.

▲ *This little girl is the proud owner of a beautifully worked silver rattle complete with bells, coral teething stick and whistle. As it is so precious, it is attached to her waist by a silver chain.*

▼ *Originally this silver rattle would have hung from the ring. A ribbon tied to the ring would have been attached to the mother's girdle or belt.*

PRICE GUIDE ❹

◄ *A far less ornate style of rattle, this is a Georgian example in silver. Again it has a whistle and bells, but the teething stick is in ivory.*

PRICE GUIDE ❻

▲ *A rather elaborate early Regency silver rattle with bells and a whistle. The coral teething stick was a common feature of rattles of this period.*

PRICE GUIDE ❼

▶ *Rattles came in many shapes and styles; this silver shell is dangling from an ivory teething ring.*

PRICE GUIDE ❹

virtuoso feats of craftsmanship. The finest rattles were embellished with elaborate chasing, pierced-work done with a hacksaw, and bright-cut engraved decoration executed with a double-edged tool that cut and polished the metal at the same time.

CORAL COMFORTER

Many rattles are made in rather dagger- or flute-like shapes, reflecting the fact that they combined several functions. The most common arrangement was to mount the metallic body of the rattle on a stem of ivory or, even more often, coral. One or two rows of little bells wound round the body, and its far end consisted of a hollow mouthpiece for use as a whistle. The pinkness of the coral added a nice touch of colour to a silver or silver-gilt rattle, but the main reason for choosing this material was that it provided the baby with a teething stick to gnaw at when the first teeth were coming through. It was believed that the coral cooled the baby's sore gums as well as acting as a dummy, and there was also a tradition that the substance had magical protective powers against the Evil Eye and other dangers. Whatever the advantages or otherwise of this kind of 'pacifier', it was certainly preferable to many other common practices such as giving babies sponges soaked in rum to suck!

Victorian craftsmen continued to make rattles in silver, but they were also mass-produced in a variety of materials including mother-of-pearl, wood and tin. If 19th-century versions of rococo were on the heavy side, the Victorians compensated with characteristic exuberance by incorporating dolls, clowns, Mr Punch, rabbits and a variety of other human and animal figures that give their babies' rattles a special charm of their own.

Royal Rattles

SOME OF THE MOST BEAUTIFUL RATTLES WHICH HAVE SURVIVED TO THE PRESENT DAY WERE THOSE GIVEN TO ROYAL CHILDREN. THE EXQUISITE SILVER FILIGREE RATTLE (LEFT) WAS A PRESENT GIVEN TO THE NURSERY OF GEORGE IV WHEN HE WAS SIX. THE MORE ELABORATE SILVER-GILT RATTLE COMPLETE WITH BELLS, WHISTLE AND CORAL COMFORTER, WAS USED BY QUEEN VICTORIA.

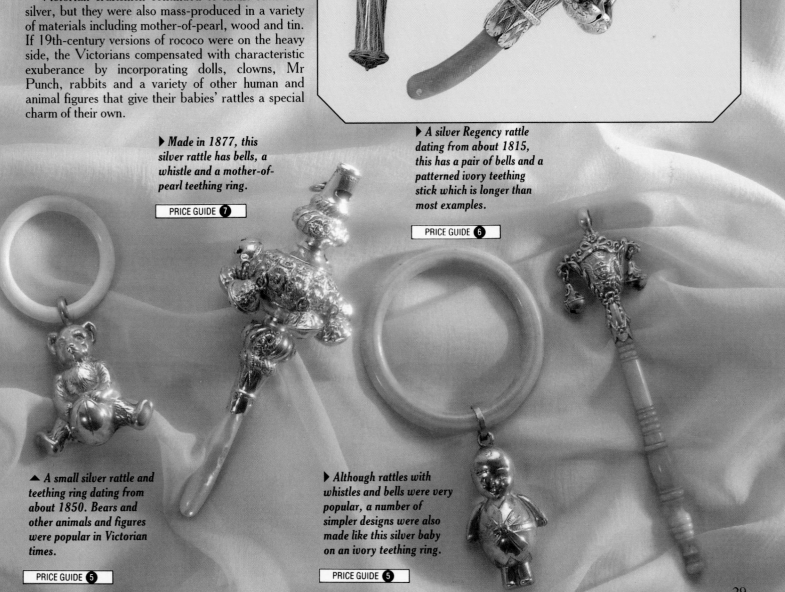

▶ Made in 1877, this silver rattle has bells, a whistle and a mother-of-pearl teething ring.

PRICE GUIDE **7**

▶ A silver Regency rattle dating from about 1815, this has a pair of bells and a patterned ivory teething stick which is longer than most examples.

PRICE GUIDE **6**

▲ A small silver rattle and teething ring dating from about 1850. Bears and other animals and figures were popular in Victorian times.

PRICE GUIDE **5**

▶ Although rattles with whistles and bells were very popular, a number of simpler designs were also made like this silver baby on an ivory teething ring.

PRICE GUIDE **5**

Regency Toys

Regency children grew up with a rapidly
expanding range of toys and games –
from tin soldiers and Noah's Arks to
jigsaw puzzles and toy theatres

Many Regency toys, from the crudest to the
most exquisitely carved and painted, were
made of wood. Even poor children might
own a simple wheeled pull-along toy. In the richest
households, the wooden rocking horse was king of
the nursery. By comparison with later examples, the
Regency rocking horse was an energetic steed, with
legs at full gallop and head outstretched.

On Sundays, the Regency child might be found at
an altogether more sedate game of lining up Noah
and his animals before a smart wooden Ark. In pious
households, re-enacting the great biblical story of the
Flood was considered the only decent form of play
for Sundays. Each small wooden figure was pain-
stakingly carved and painted. As well as Noah and
his family, up to 30 different species of animals
would be marshalled up the ramp.

PLAYING AT SOLDIERS

On any other day, sets of wooden soldiers might be
seen marching across the nursery floor. The military
exploits of Frederick the Great had already created a
new fashion for toy soldiers in the late 18th century.
Flat figures made of tin, appropriately painted, were
made in large numbers from about 1775 onwards.
Complete armies could thus be assembled and put
through their paces in games of strategy and military
manoeuvres. Cheaper cardboard soldiers mounted
on small wooden blocks appeared in the early 19th
century.

▼ *A painted Noah's Ark,
complete with its wooden
animals, dating from
around 1830.*

The early 19th century also saw the appearance of
tin plate toys, brightly painted in enamel colours.
These toys took many forms, from dolls' house
furniture to intricate circus sets complete with a ring,
acrobats and prancing horses.

TOY THEATRE

A prominent new fashion in the Regency nursery
was the toy theatre, which reflected the early 19th-
century fashion for the theatre in the adult world.
The idea of a miniature theatre, complete with script
and characters, was commercialized by William
West in 1812. The characters took the form of
engravings on paper which were supplied in sheets
and which the children themselves pasted on to a
board and cut out. The cheapest sets were printed in
black and white, and the more expensive ones in
colour.

These toy theatre characters were characteristically depicted in the most melodramatic poses. They
'performed' the drama against backdrops appropriate for each scene, which were also supplied as
engravings.

The script was adapted and condensed from an
actual play. As the drama unfolded, the characters
were pushed on to the stage and pulled off again at
the appropriate moment by means of wire slides.
Popular plays for the toy theatre included *Beauty*

◀ Painted wooden toys were prolific in Regency times and varied greatly from elaborate rocking horses to a simple wooden donkey or learning bricks painted with animals and letters. Some toys reflected the latest trends at the time, such as toy theatres. The circus was an exciting form of entertainment and many a child would have been delighted with a pull-along lion tamer and his ferocious beast.

▼ Dolls were well-loved Regency toys. Wood was a popular material and wooden dolls were often hand carved and painted. By the early 1800s, the first wax dolls appeared and these would have actual tufts of hair rather than painted hair. Papier-mâché dolls, like the harlequin, were stuffed with kid or linen, but because they were softer they often did not withstand the rough and tumble of nursery life.

manufacture of the jigsaw itself and its box.

Board games, like jigsaw puzzles, also tended to serve the moral edification of the Regency child. In 'The Game of Human Life', for instance, issued in 1790 and still popular in the early 19th century, players threw dice to progress along a route punctuated with moral dangers, temptations and difficulties.

Less heavily moralistic board games were devised on a number of diverse themes, although an opportunity to educate was not easily missed. 'The Noble Game of the Elephant and Castle, or Travelling in Asia', published in London in 1822, consisted of 24 scenes picturesquely imposed upon the body of an elephant and his mahout, giving a subtle geography lesson.

OUTDOOR GAMES

Not all childish amusement was to be had in the confines of the nursery. Outdoors, physical energy could be worked off astride a hobby horse. On a sunny day, out would come the hoops and the shuttlecocks, the spinning tops, the skipping ropes and the marbles and, on a windy day, kites.

Team games were many and various. As today, children could be seen playing rounders, cricket and hopscotch. Other outdoor games included Harry Racket (hide and seek), Hoodman Blind (blind man's buff) and tittermetrotter (see-saw). Then there was Hunt the Hare, Conquering Lobs, Pig in the Ring and Puss in the Corner.

Back in the nursery, the latest inventions and discoveries contributed to the development of new toys such as wooden or tin toy trains, which

and the Beast, Blue Beard, The Grand Melodrama of the Broken Sword, The Brigand and *The Casket of Gloriana*. In all, 300 different plays were adapted for the miniature theatre.

Printsellers, the main suppliers of sheets for the toy theatre, also provided amusements such as jigsaw puzzles, board games and playing cards. The jigsaw puzzle was invented by John Spilsbury, an engraver and map-maker, in about 1760. The 'dissected puzzle', as the jigsaw was then known, was simply a dissected map designed to teach children geography in an entertaining manner.

THE POPULAR PUZZLE

Following the success of John Spilsbury's initial invention, jigsaws in the form of scientific and historical tables soon followed. The latter consisted of portraits of the kings and queens of England, starting with William I; each reign was annotated with its own list of 'Remarkable Events and Eminent Persons'. Religious jigsaw puzzles were also popular and illustrated stories from the Bible or recounted mind-improving moral tales.

The pictures on jigsaw puzzles were hand-coloured lithographs. These were initially mounted on mahogany and the jigsaw itself sold in a mahogany box with a sliding lid. Whitewood, a cheaper substitute, soon replaced mahogany both for the

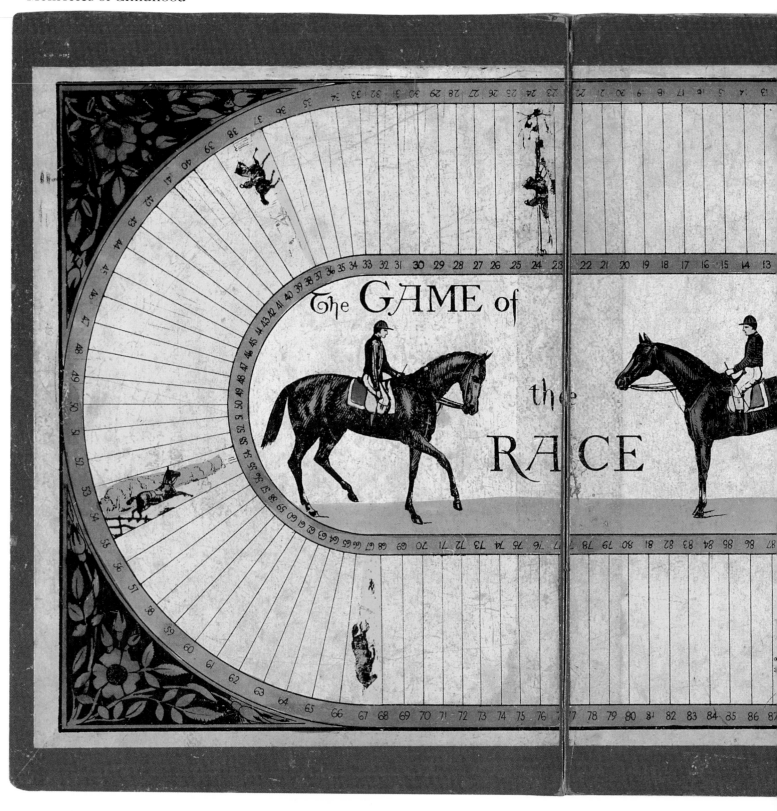

▲ *Simulating a steeplechase for any number of players, this 19th century English board game uses two dice, counters, a horse and jockey and a set of obstacles (fences, waterjumps and a gate).*

appeared at the very end of the Regency period. As Stephenson's Rocket first ran on 15th September 1830, a toy train was almost as much of a novelty as its real-life model.

The moving-picture toy, which made its appearance in 1825, exploited the phenomenon of the persistence of vision. Viewed in rapid succession, a series of drawings of, say, a hopping frog, or galloping horse, in progressive stages of movement, gave the illusion of movement itself. Various mechanical devices for passing these images quickly before the eyes were developed. One of the most effective was the Phenakistiscope. This consisted of a disc

with as many as 20 drawings; spinning the disc produced the illusion of a moving image.

MISCELLANEOUS MATERIALS

Although wood, paper and metal were the principal materials for Regency toys, a small number of toys were made from various other materials. French prisoners of war passed their time in captivity by making dominoes, painted boxes and spillikins out of mutton bones. They also made straw-work Noah's Arks. Glass was also used for a whole range of miniature objects intended to be treated as toys. They took many forms including hats, swords, bells,

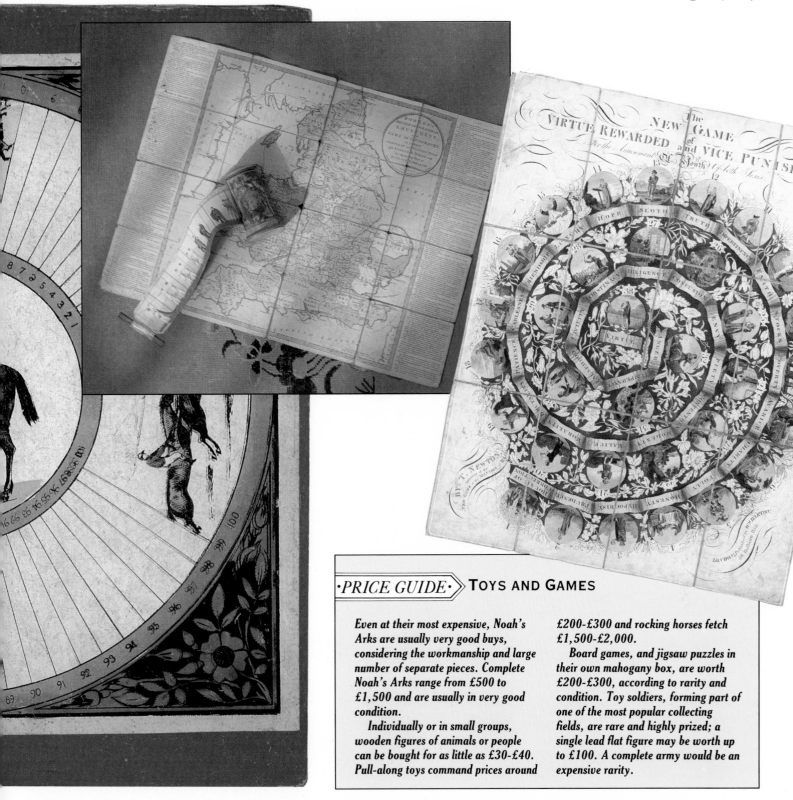

human and animal figures as well as many other shapes besides.

COLLECTING TOYS AND GAMES
The field of antique toys is as large as it is diverse and collectors therefore tend to specialize. Besides dolls and their houses and belongings, the main collecting areas are model soldiers, the toy theatre, jigsaw puzzles and board games – often using dice and counters beautifully carved from mother-of-pearl, bone and ivory. Whatever the moral attitude towards dicing, board games were played enthusiastically. Small wooden, tinplate, glass or plaster

figures of animals and people were also popular.

Although Regency toys are much rarer than later 19th- and 20th-century examples, they appear quite frequently at auction. Specialist dealers in early toys are, however, very few and far between these days.

Board games and jigsaw puzzles are best displayed under glass, away from strong sunlight to preserve their colours. An army of soldiers or group of animals from a Noah's Ark or toy circus are most effective when arranged in authentic-looking formation. Most Regency toys are too precious to be mended by the amateur and should be taken to a professional restorer.

▲▲ *Games were not only fun but educational too, like the* Game of Geography *which plots a tour through Great Britain. Others like* Virtue Rewarded *and* Vice Punished *have obvious moral overtones.*

The Rocking Horse

The rocking horse was known as the king of toys and often took pride of place in the centre of the boy's bedroom, poised ready for the many adventures and imaginary exploits of years to come

For playing indoors on a rainy day or whiling away lonely hours, there was no better toy than a rocking horse. Too large to be put away in the toy cupboard, the rocking horse stood ever ready, in the middle of a boy's bedroom or neatly placed along a wall, to take his young rider on yet another imaginary journey of adventure.

EARLY BEGINNINGS

The origins of the rocking horse, one of the most exciting of all toys, go back over 300 years. From its very beginnings, it was designated to be the coveted toy of only the children of wealthier families. Its realistic appearance and motion, and above all the fact that it could actually be ridden, made it infinitely more desirable than the humble hobby horse. Although, for obvious reasons, rocking horses could never be made by machine, improved production methods introduced during the 19th century made them more affordable and more common-place in less wealthy households. Thus the rocking horse, the king of toys, had become a central figure in many a nursery or bedroom of the 1920s and 1930s.

The rocking horse is thought to have originated in the 17th century. The idea of a wooden horse large enough for a child to ride on may have developed from the saddle tree or 'horse' used to hold saddlery and armour. When not in use, it was doubtless irresistible as an imaginary mount for children keen to emulate the horsemanship of their elders.

THE BOAT-SHAPED HORSE

The earliest rocking horses had a boat-shaped structure which consisted of two parallel semi-circular slabs of wood held vertically by a small seat placed between them. The horse's head, carved out of solid wood, was mounted in front of the seat and counterbalanced by a solid wood 'rump' behind. For comfort, foot-rests were fitted to the semi-circular rockers and, for safety, the ends of the rockers were counter-turned to prevent the horse rocking right over. Life-like touches might include a real horsehair mane and tail and a small dummy pistol in a holster carved out of the wood at the horse's neck.

Other rocking horses of this early, boat-

shaped type sometimes had legs carved in relief on the sides of the rockers, and sported a splendidly flowing mane and tail carved out of the solid wood. Like the tails of real horses of the period, the rocking horse's tail might be plaited and secured with a ribbon. These rocking horses were probably not painted. They show no signs of having worn a bridle, although their young riders probably made reins out of leather or string.

By the late 17th century, rocking horses were being made with free-standing legs fixed to a wooden platform that was in turn attached to a pair of bow-shaped rockers. They had a strutting rather than galloping

▲ By the 1930s the most popular design for rocking horses was a trestle mount rather than the more traditional bow rocker. Apart from this basic change most other design features of the horse remained remarkably similar to those of rocking horses made since the end of the 18th century. Dapple grey horses were as popular as ever.

posture and were given realistic leather saddles and bridles.

GALLOPING HORSES

The galloping rocking horse on bow-shaped rockers probably originated in the late 18th century, and remained the standard type right through to the 1880s. These rocking horses were realistically carved both in general outline and in fine detail. They often had pricked ears, an open mouth and flared nostrils, with the head extended forward, as if they were racing. Some were also painted, most often in what had come to be thought of as the classic dapple grey, with black patches on the legs and black hooves. Colour was also used to pick out the mouth, nostrils, eyes and ears. The most prized horses sported manes and tails of luxuriant white horsehair and wore finely crafted leather bridles and saddles, sometimes with the addition of a fabric or leather saddle-cloth.

By the early 19th century, rocking horses were being advertised by manufacturers as desirable toys for children of both sexes. One London toymaker, William Kain, advertised 'Elegant Rocking Horses with Improv'd Manes & Tails'. Another, William West, supplied 'New Rocking Horses for Children', among which were 'My Own Rocking Horse' for a boy, and 'My Favorite Rocking Horse' for a girl. It was subtly indicated, however, that while little boys were permitted to gallop furiously astride, hell for leather, little girls were expected to ride demurely side-saddle. Some rocking horses were even fitted with a small wicker chair so that girls could rock with decorum.

Rocking horses of the 18th and early 19th century tended to be rather narrow, with steep bow rockers and irregular spots. However, as the 19th century progressed, they became broader and their rockers less steep. Necks and heads were held high and dapples assumed a more regular pattern.

THE TRESTLE

Attractive though the horse on its bow rockers was, the possibility of its rocking right over when ridden too enthusiastically made it somewhat unsafe for the boisterous child. Even the counter-turned ends of the rockers did not always prevent mishaps occurring when the horse was ridden furiously. In the 1880s, a safer platform was devised and the rocking motion formerly provided by the curved rockers was replaced by a gentler horizontal movement back and forth. The horse's legs were attached to a pair of planks which swung on metal brackets mounted each end of a trestle-like structure.

After about 1890, progressively more rocking horses were mounted on a trestle stand of this type. As well as making for a safer ride, trestle-mounted rocking horses took up less space than bow-mounted ones, and they did not move about, mark the floor or gouge holes in walls or furniture. For all that, however, bow rockers are still the more attractive model, with nothing to spoil the clean lines of the horse's prancing legs.

▲ *Original rocking horses are often bought as more than just playthings – they are regarded as very pleasing pieces of furniture in their own right.*

▼ *This splendid rocking horse on a hinged trestle rocker actually belonged to Her Royal Highness The Princess Royal.*

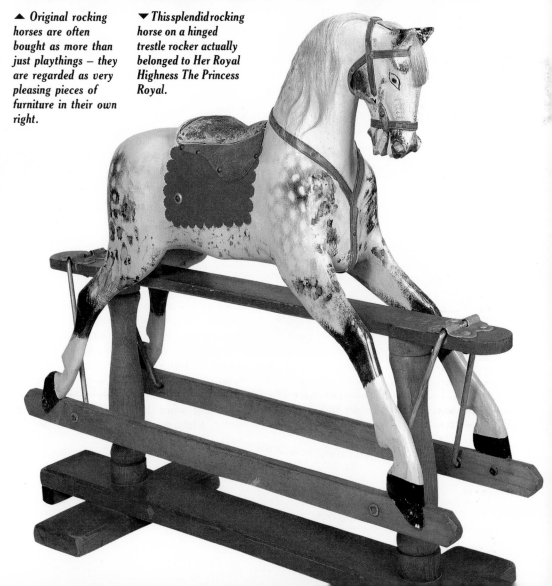

The Victorian Rocking Horse

THE VICTORIAN ERA WAS A GOLDEN AGE FOR TOYS. DUE TO THE RAPID EXPANSION OF TOY MANUFACTURERS THERE WAS A WIDER VARIETY OF MOST TOYS AVAILABLE INCLUDING THE LONG-CHERISHED ROCKING HORSE.

A FINE EXAMPLE OF THE POPULAR DAPPLED GREY ROCKING HORSE, THIS MODEL WAS MADE IN THE LATE 19TH CENTURY FROM CARVED WOOD AND IS MOUNTED ON A LARGE BOW ROCKER.

FITTED WITH A REALISTIC BROWN LEATHER BRIDLE AND SADDLE, THE HORSE EVEN HAS METAL STIRRUPS ATTACHED. A TOUCH OF AUTHENTICITY IS ALSO ADDED BY THE GLORIOUS LONG MANE OF BLACK HAIR WHICH COVERS THE HORSE'S HEAD AND NECK, AND WHICH ALSO MAKES THE TAIL.

① AFTER SANDING, GESSO AND PAINT WERE ADDED WITH A COAT OF VARNISH.

② FINELY CRAFTED LEATHER WAS USED FOR SADDLES.

③ REAL HORSES' HAIR IS USED FOR THE MANE.

④ HOOVES ARE FIRMLY NAILED TO THE BASE.

Fine Carving

DISPLAYED FLARED NOSTRILS AND OPEN MOUTH, BOTH OF WHICH HAVE BEEN DELICATELY CARVED BY HAND.

The Modern Horse

THIS MODERN HORSE HAS BEEN MADE IN A VERY SIMILAR DESIGN TO THE VICTORIAN ROCKING HORSE. IT WAS MADE USING 80 YEAR-OLD ASH WHICH IS LEFT IN ITS NATURAL COLOUR.

The design of the classic dapple grey rocking horse portrays a certain timelessness. Its appearance remained as unchanged through time as the method of its manufacture. The body was built up with as many as a dozen separate blocks of wood – usually pine or beech – roughly carved to the appropriate shape and either glued or tenoned together. After further filing and sanding, the horse was painted with gesso to smooth over the joints, followed by a coat of white paint, the grey dapples and varnish. When it had been fixed to its rockers or trestle, the horse was given its mane and tail, and the saddle and bridle were then added.

The first commercial manufacturers of rocking horses were probably the makers of fairground gallopers. Such firms also made life-size wooden horses for saddlers and supplied wooden horses's heads for use as public house signs. The firm of G. and J. Lines began making rocking horses in this way in the

·PRICE GUIDE·

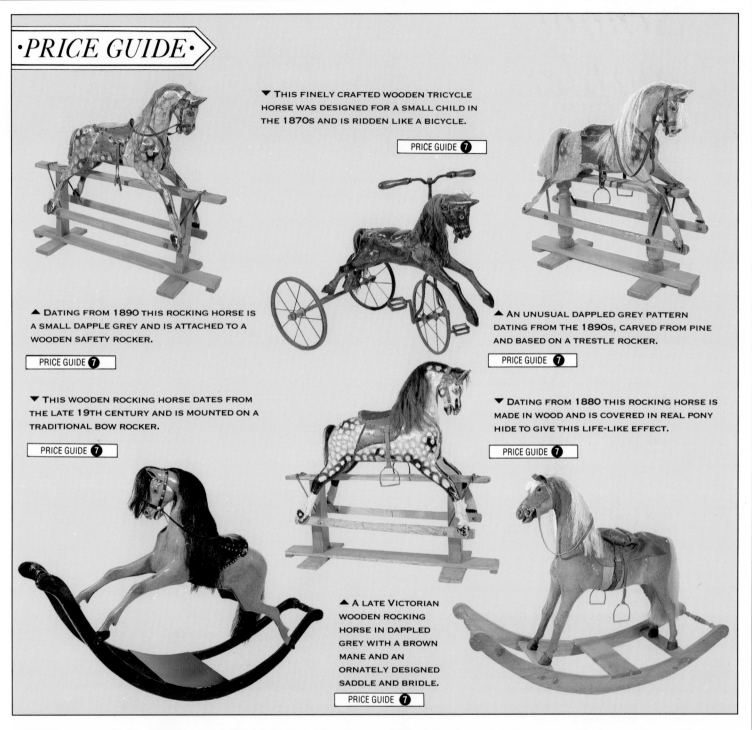

▼ THIS FINELY CRAFTED WOODEN TRICYCLE HORSE WAS DESIGNED FOR A SMALL CHILD IN THE 1870S AND IS RIDDEN LIKE A BICYCLE.

PRICE GUIDE ❼

▲ DATING FROM 1890 THIS ROCKING HORSE IS A SMALL DAPPLE GREY AND IS ATTACHED TO A WOODEN SAFETY ROCKER.

PRICE GUIDE ❼

▲ AN UNUSUAL DAPPLED GREY PATTERN DATING FROM THE 1890S, CARVED FROM PINE AND BASED ON A TRESTLE ROCKER.

PRICE GUIDE ❼

▼ THIS WOODEN ROCKING HORSE DATES FROM THE LATE 19TH CENTURY AND IS MOUNTED ON A TRADITIONAL BOW ROCKER.

PRICE GUIDE ❼

▼ DATING FROM 1880 THIS ROCKING HORSE IS MADE IN WOOD AND IS COVERED IN REAL PONY HIDE TO GIVE THIS LIFE-LIKE EFFECT.

PRICE GUIDE ❼

▲ A LATE VICTORIAN WOODEN ROCKING HORSE IN DAPPLED GREY WITH A BROWN MANE AND AN ORNATELY DESIGNED SADDLE AND BRIDLE.

PRICE GUIDE ❼

mid-19th century. By the 1920s and 1930, G. and J. Lines, alongside their off-shoot Lines Bros Ltd, were making a range that included old-style rocking horses on bow rockers, 'combination' horses on wheels that would also be lifted on and off rockers, horses with medieval-style trappings on which little boys might play at jousting or lead a crusade, and quantities of the classic dapple greys on their safe trestle stands.

Other notable manufacturers of the period included the Liver-pool Toy Industry, Woodrow & Co. of London, and Norton & Baker of Birmingham. Along with the horses made by the two Lines firms, it would have been their rocking horses that were found in the toy departments of large department stores such as Gamages and Selfridges.

Unfortunately, even with 1920s rocking horses, it is difficult to attribute a particular horse to its maker. Few makers stamped their work and, even if they had, later repainting or refurbishing is likely to have obliterated the identification.

Continuing a tradition that was carried on through generations, makers of rocking horses were not greatly affected by the radical new designs of the 1920s and 1930s; these were for the adult world rather than the nursery.

POINTS TO WATCH

■ After soundness of construction, one of the most important features of a rocking horse is a good head; the eyes should be well defined, the ears pricked and the nostrils proudly flared.

■ Ideally, the paintwork should be original, as should the saddle, bridle straps and stirrups.

■ The mane and tail, which should be luxuriant rather than straggly, should be of real horse hair. Also check that they are firmly secured.

■ In an old or antique piece, superficial damage, such as a chip to the ears, is almost to be expected and is not regarded as a major flaw.

■ 3-footed rocking horses on trestles are sought-after.

School Samplers

The many hours of toiling over alphabet, number and motto samplers through the ages have left today's collector with a splendid legacy

Personal collections of stitches and patterns have been embroidered for hundreds of years by both adults and children. These collections are called samplers – from the Old French *essamplaire* or *exemplaire,* meaning a pattern which could be copied – and they form a unique and collectable record of domestic needlework from the 15th century to the present day.

Samplers were worked primarily as a learning process to try out different stitches, techniques and patterns which could then be used as reference material for the accomplished stitcher. The earliest written reference occurs in 1502, when the account book of Elizabeth of York shows the purchase of 'lynnyn cloth for a sampler'.

IN THE BEGINNING

Early samplers show realistic and fanciful designs of flowers, fruit, animals, birds and figures as well as border patterns. Many of these designs were copied from printed pattern books originating in Europe and later printed in England. The samplers were worked on linen fabric or fine canvas using silk, linen or wool threads and they employed a variety of stitches and techniques, including cutwork and drawn thread-work, metal-thread embroidery and beading. Later samplers, particularly those produced during the 18th and 19th centuries, show an increasing use of alphabets and moral and religious verses.

During the 19th century, most samplers were stitched by young girls in schools and orphanages as part of their general education. These school samplers fall into two distinct categories: embroidered samplers and plain sewing samplers.

EMBROIDERED SAMPLERS

Embroidered samplers, based on the alphabet, not only taught pupils the skill of embroidery, but also their letters and spelling. Girls would often go into service after leaving school, and to have a good standard of spelling and needlework meant that they could hope to avoid the menial jobs in the kitchens and aspire to become a lady's maid. In service, a lady's maid spent much of her time marking the household linen with embroidered names, numbers and monograms, so neatness of stitching and good spelling were essential.

Girls usually worked one complete alphabet sampler per year during their schooldays, and in most schools the teacher would keep a needlework exercise book to show the progress of her pupils.

38

◀ *Alphabets and numbers, mottos and religious texts were all staple subjects for Victorian stitch samplers. The majority of 19th-century examples were actually made by young schoolgirls who often displayed extraordinary skill in needlework. Today, samplers are extremely collectable and the great demand for them has led to rather high prices.*

▼ *A simple prayer from a 13-year-old girl forms the basis of this pretty, pastel sampler. It is worked entirely in cross-stitch which lends itself perfectly to creating the stylized forms of the flowers and trees in this design.*

Many of these books have survived intact, showing tiny examples of each child's work, stitched or pinned to the pages.

In addition to embroidery, samples of knitting, crochet, patchwork and plain sewing were included. A typical book of this kind was worked by pupils of the Westbourne Union School, Sussex, during the years 1842 to 1844. Each page of work is headed by a strip of canvas showing the girl's name and age worked in cross-stitch.

CROSS-STITCH SAMPLERS

Most embroidered samplers consist of one or two simple alphabets and numerals enclosed within a narrow border, usually worked in coloured cross-stitch on coarse woollen tammy or, occasionally, on linen. Ordinary cross-stitch and marking cross-stitch – which is the same on both sides of the fabric – are, in general, the only stitches used on this type of sampler. The date of completion, and the names and age of the stitcher were usually added. More complex samplers were produced, some containing as many as 20 different alphabets in varying sizes, and moral verses, religious texts and tiny motifs of houses, animals and flowers were also included.

As well as embroidery, plain sewing was taught

◀ *The haphazardly arranged stitch patterns on random samplers were used as 'try-outs' for different designs and techniques. The example (far left), dated 1847, contrasts sharply with the very formalized alphabet sampler (left) which is especially attractive with its variegated letters.*

▼ *Small sections of Victorian stitchwork are still often found where they were always kept – in 19th-century workboxes.*

along the lines laid down by various manuals produced for use in educational establishments. *Plain needlework in all its branches,* published in 1849 for use in the National Industrial School of the Holy Trinity at Finchley, states the need for all women to have 'a practical acquaintance with needlework. . . . this is more particularly the case with reference to females in humble life, whether with a view to domestic neatness and economy, or to profitable occupation in a pecuniary light.' The curriculum lists 12 basic stitches which were 'practised upon the Third-Class Sampler, and then they are all done upon the Second-Class Sampler'.

The samplers were worked on white linen or cotton with white or neutral threads. They illustrate the full range of techniques used to create both domestic and household linen. The fabric was firstly hemmed, then cut and darned extremely neatly. Buttonholes, covered buttons, hooks, eyes and fabric tags and tapes were added, as well as types of shaping such as tucks and gathers. Advanced samplers demonstrated the different methods of making seams, inserting collars and cuffs and almost invisible patching.

On the whole, plain sewing samplers show exquisite workmanship and many include some kind of decorative stitching such as cutwork, drawn threadwork and faggoting. Some samplers are signed and dated, usually in cross-stitch or chain-stitch.

TIPS FOR THE COLLECTOR

Textiles in general, particularly samplers, are becoming increasingly attractive to collectors due to their highly personal nature. Nineteenth century samplers can be found at most antique fairs and markets, usually on specialist textile stalls.

Embroidered samplers are generally framed and should be reframed using an acid-free backing board and a filet of the same board to keep the embroidery and the glass apart. The fabric must be in good condition, but minor repairs are possible.

Contact a local museum for advice before attempting to clean an embroidered sampler, as the embroidery may not be colourfast. Plain sewing samplers are usually more sturdy and will respond to careful hand-washing.

◀ *Band samplers, recognizable by their strip-like format, were used to show border patterns which could be used on items of clothing or domestic linens. The embroidered designs themselves were usually rather dense, with narrow spaces in between. This sampler, from Belgium, uses mainly cross-stitch.*

⟨·*PRICE GUIDE*·⟩

SCHOOL SAMPLERS

As the majority of Victorian samplers are dated, this will affect the asking price, together with the size, amount of stitching and condition. Expect to pay between £300 and £750 for a detailed alphabet sampler, framed and in excellent condition.

A small sampler showing one or two alphabets can cost from around £150.

Unframed examples may be cheaper, but check that repeated folding has not frayed the fabric or stitching, and that the outer edge is not badly damaged.

The price of plain sewing samplers, depending on date and complexity, can be as low as £40 to £60, but a detailed example could cost in the region of £100 to buy.

The Victorian Schoolroom

Functionally furnished with rows of wooden desks and chairs, a
blackboard and glowing stove, the village school was always alive
with the chant of children's voices

The Victorian village school was very different
from the sophisticated classrooms of today.
With few funds to rely on, there were no
printed charts or diagrams, but instead the walls
were brightened with colourful pictures by the pupils
themselves. Equipment was minimal and functional,
dominated by the rows of desks and benches. Very
often all the local boys and girls, aged between three
and fourteen, crowded into this single room, their
separate lessons creating a confused hubub of half-
remembered facts and undigested sums.

Deprived and neglected though the village schoolroom appears to modern eyes, it was certainly not
cheerless. A caring and dedicated master or mistress, allied to the indomitable high spirits of the
pupils, could transform the somewhat overcrowded,
under-equipped schoolroom into a place of fellow-
ship, excitement and genuine learning. To many, it
offered a place to meet and make friends and a
welcome escape from the drudgery of home life.

*A corner of a
Victorian
schoolroom
showing
essential
teaching
equipment
from globes of
the world,
which would
be handed
around the
class, to the
lined
blackboard,
abacus,
3-dimensional
geometric
forms to the
teacher's
cane.*

41

Monday, 8.50am. A bell on the schoolhouse roof rings noisily and insistently, and the children milling in the dusty street form a restless line outside the door. Ten minutes later the bell rings a second time, and the door is opened from within by the monitor, a boy of 12. The infants – up to the age of six – hurry to their own special room. Older children, from frail girls of seven to shambling, half-grown farm boys, squeeze between the backless benches and the long desks which are ranged like church pews in the main classroom.

The schoolroom is a dark, unattractive room, though the children see it for what it represents to them. For some, it is little more than a place to be, neither better nor worse than the farm or domestic work awaiting them, but for others it is a room of hope and opportunity, offering an escape from the ignorance and hardship of working-class rural life.

THE SCHOOLROOM

Many so-called 'village schools' were built for poor country children after the 1870 Education Act which sought to bring some kind of uniformity to existing church and charity schools. The Act tried to enforce the building of schools by rural district councils so that every child was within two miles of a school, although in practice this was not always possible.

A new, purpose-built schoolhouse generally consisted of one large, rectangular room, with maybe a smaller room for the infants if the council could afford it. Otherwise, the little children might sit in a gallery at one end of the schoolroom, their desks raised on steps so that the master or mistress could keep an eye on them. Most schools were overcrowded. Officially each student was allocated a minimum area, but frequently this inadequate standard was ignored.

The walls were simply whitewashed as funds from schoolboard or church authority were small. This meant that repairs and redecoration were rarely carried out with any urgency. More than one child had to squeeze along his bench to avoid the drip of a leaky roof when missing slates opened the ceiling to the sky.

▲ *School days were, on the whole, uncomfortable and boring. Large numbers of children were crammed into small, badly-lit rooms and lessons consisted of merely learning by rote.*

▶ *With its colourful wooden beads, the ball frame, or abacus, was a practical and entertaining way for children to learn numbers.*

▼ *Prayers, an important part of the Victorian school day, were traditionally said after morning assembly. This sketch shows girls from a Whitechapel school at prayer.*

The narrow windows were purposely high so that children could not gaze longingly at the world outside. As a result, natural light was poor and often barely adequate for working. Unfortunately, this was rarely supplemented by gas lighting, which had reached most city schools by the late 19th century, but was still a luxury in many poorer country areas.

SEATING AND HEATING

Children generally sat on backless benches fixed to the floor. Since their long desks were also fixed, the result was that few sat comfortably unless fortunate enough to be of the appropriate size.

There were other disadvantages to this type of furniture arrangement. An extraordinary commotion was created, for example, when a child, late for school, had to squeeze past fellow pupils or go to relieve himself in the 'offices', as the primitive school toilets were called. School inspectors regularly complained about this inefficient and uncomfortable way of seating, but the extra expense of individual desks made most school managers think twice before investing in such luxuries as 'the dual improved Hallamshire convertible desks, three feet six inches long, pitch pine, varnished, and to include porcelain inkwells; 19s 6d each.'

LIFE AND LEISURE
Teacher Training

ANYONE COULD TAKE UP A POSITION AS A SCHOOLTEACHER UNTIL THE INTRODUCTION OF THE PUPIL TEACHER SYSTEM IN 1846. A TEACHER THEN HAD TO WORK THROUGH THE RANKS IN A LABORIOUS APPRENTICESHIP. AGED 12, A BRIGHT YOUNG BOY OR GIRL COULD BECOME A MONITOR OR TEACHING ASSISTANT.

THE REAL APPRENTICESHIP BEGAN AT 13, WITH THE PROMOTION TO PUPIL TEACHER — FIVE ARDUOUS YEARS OF TEACHING.

THIS COURSE LED TO THE QUEEN'S SCHOLARSHIP EXAMINATION, WHERE THE SUCCESSFUL CANDIDATE WON A PLACE ON A REAL TEACHER TRAINING COURSE; WITH A SECOND- OR THIRD-CLASS QUALIFICATION, HE OR SHE COULD RETURN TO THEIR SCHOOL AS AN ASSISTANT MASTER/MISTRESS.

▲ POOR SOCIAL CONDITIONS AND OVERCROWDING FREQUENTLY RESULTED IN UNRULY BEHAVIOUR. MAINTAINING DISCIPLINE WAS OFTEN A MAJOR PART OF THE TEACHER'S JOB AND MOST RESORTED TO THE CANE FOR OFFENCES SUCH AS FIGHTING.

▶ MANY VICTORIAN TEACHERS WERE WOMEN. AT FIRST THEY WERE MAINLY WORKING-CLASS GIRLS, WHO BEGAN AS PUPIL TEACHERS, BUT LATER, AS THE DEMAND FOR TEACHERS GREW, MIDDLE-CLASS WOMEN BECAME ATTRACTED TO THE PROFESSION.

below freezing. And unless the teacher or assistant lit the fire long before school opened, classes might just as well have been held outside. 'The thermometer stands at 24½ degrees F, 10 o'clock, fires lighted 2½ hours,' wrote one despairing Devon master in his weekly log book. And on another occasion: 'children obliged to exercise to keep warm'. On wet days children draped their soaking coats over the tall fireguard to dry, thus absorbing what little heat was available.

EDUCATIONAL EQUIPMENT

Most schoolmasters could rely on using the large blackboard mounted on an easel, with which every schoolroom was equipped, although there were exceptions. One hard-pressed West Country master wrote: 'I have not given a blackboard lesson of any sort, on account of having no chalk.'

The students practised writing on a variety of implements. Infants often had shallow trays of sand in which they scratched letters and numbers with a pointed stick. This had the advantage – and the disadvantage – of being quick to erase. Older students graduated to individual slates on which they took dictation and did their sums. In theory, they wiped their slates clean with a cloth brought from home, but forgetful children had frequent recourse to spit and a sleeve.

Only the most advanced students, the 10- to 12-year-olds in Standards V, VI and VII, moved on to pen and ink. These privileged few practised their

▲▶ Slates and slate pencils were standard school equipment for juniors in most schools, and were used for practising simple writing and sums. Some deeper slates could also be used as sand trays, where smaller children could practise drawing letters and numbers with their fingers. Once the rudiments of writing and arithmetic had been mastered, pupils would graduate to pen and paper.

One Essex school board even reverted from desks back to benches in order to accommodate as many children as cheaply as possible – although the minimum recommended seating was 45 cm/18in per person. Towards the end of the century, school inspectors and educational reformers won the case for separate desks. However, to begin with these were often the 'dual' variety with places for two students.

Even in the best-equipped schools, heating was a perennial problem. The open fire or cast-iron stove that provided all the heat for the schoolroom was pitifully inadequate when the temperature went

approved copperplate handwriting on real paper in their copy books. Ink was distributed by an 'ink monitor', who filled the students' individual inkwells – perhaps from a stoneware bottle of 'Stephen's Blue Black Writing Fluid' – and who washed out the inkwells on Friday afternoon. Students made pen wipers from circles of felt sewn together at the centre. Lead pencils only arrived in many country schools at the end of the century.

LOOK AND LEARN

Apart from the blackboard, there were few teaching aids. A map of Britain might hang beside a picture of King John signing the Magna Carta. Fortunate schools had a few informative wall charts of trees, birds or historical subjects, such as Roman Walls and Roads or The Battle of Hastings.

◀ IN PERSPECTIVE ▶

State Education

FOR POOR FAMILIES UP TO THE MID-19TH CENTURY, ONLY DAME AND SUNDAY SCHOOLS EXISTED. FROM 1862 AN ANNUAL VISIT OF HM INSPECTORS REWARDED GOOD RE-SULTS WITH A GRANT, KNOWN AS PAYMENT BY RESULTS. THE EDUCATION ACT IN 1870 LED TO THE FIRST STATE SCHOOLS. COMPULSORY ELEMENTARY EDUCATION WAS IN-TRODUCED IN 1880 AND BECAME FREE IN 1891.

LIFE AND LEISURE
Out-of-school Recreation

LIFE WAS NOT ALL WORK AND NO PLAY EVEN IN VICTORIAN TIMES, AND THERE WERE MANY OCCASIONS WHEN THE CHILDREN HAD TIME TO ENJOY THEM-SELVES WITH STREET GAMES OR VISITS TO LOCAL FAIRS.

ON RARE OCCASIONS, THEY EVEN WENT ON SCHOOL OUTINGS, THOUGH MANY VICTORIAN AUTHORITIES DISAPPROVED OF SCHOOL DAYS OUT FOR CHILDREN OF THE POOR. ONE SCHOOL BOARD IN DERBYSHIRE, FOR EXAMPLE, REFUSED BOLSOVER CHILDREN A DAY VISIT TO DERBY MUSEUM, FOR FEAR THAT IT MIGHT SET A PRECEDENT.

▼ MAY DAY WAS AN OCCASION FOR DRESSING UP AND GATHERING FLOWERS FOR THE MAY POLE.

CERTAIN HOLIDAYS, HOWEVER, COULD NOT BE REPRESSED. WHEREVER A CHILD LIVED, MAY DAY MEANT DRES-SING UP AND DANCING AROUND THE MAY POLE. AT LEAST ONE SCHOOL PARADED THROUGH THE TOWN, SINGING SONGS AND COLLECTING PENNIES.

ON EMPIRE DAY, 24 MAY, THE CHIL-DREN ENACTED HISTORICAL TABLEAUX, ROUNDING OFF THE PERFORMANCE WITH A SONG.

◀ TRAVELLING SIDESHOWS WERE A CONSTANT SOURCE OF EXCITEMENT AND FASCINATION FOR CHILDREN.

▼ ON NATIONAL HOLIDAYS, CHILDREN JOINED IN THE SHOWS OF PATRIOTISM.

Books for the older children were often in short supply. 'We have only a few broken Testaments to read from, no secular books of any sort,' complained one headmaster in his log book, and many of his colleagues shared his frustration.

Infants fared better, as their play equipment was relatively inexpensive. Modelling clay and beads for threading, as well as blocks and buttons, were readily available. Little children also practised knitting, and embroidered samplers, and, in many schools, could learn about numbers by using a ball frame – a simple abacus with sliding wooden beads. Alphabets and numbers often hung from the dado rail, and jars of wild flowers sometimes stood on the window sills.

Luxury items, such as a piano or even a globe, were not within the reach of most village schools, though they were sometimes the gift of a generous vicar or squire. More likely was a tuning fork to start off the morning hymn or singing lessons.

▶ *Many school children were given special tasks to perform. The 'ink monitor's' job was to mix up the ink from powder and water in large jars.*

The School Desk

Relatively few of the simple and solidly constructed school desks of the
19th century have survived, and today these functional pieces of
furniture are widely sought by collectors

The school desk is perhaps not an obvious antique, but during the latter part of the 19th century, solid, well-designed examples were produced – many just as worthy of attention as some of the more elaborate pieces designed for the home.

The familiar locker desk has been around for almost a century, yet few people have ever devoted much time to its study. This is a pity because, although simple in design and function, the school desk tells us a lot about attitudes to education and in many respects it is sad that examples of a relatively 'modern' antique can be hard to find today.

VICTORIAN EDUCATION

Structured education of the vast mass of the population came late in the Victorian era. There had, of course, been schools of various descriptions for centuries – Eton was founded by Henry VI – catering for children from a variety of backgrounds. But rarely were the schools good or supplied with furniture and equipment suitable for teaching. Even the children of fairly well-off middle class families could not be certain of receiving a proper education.

Vast tracts of the country were without schools even by the middle of the 19th century and, in areas that had them, attendance was often low and further reduced by the onset of winter when lack of boots and long distances to walk combined to keep children at home. Less inclement seasons offered other diversions. In rural areas, the all-important harvest had to be gathered and young children were pressed into service as a matter of course. In the towns, children often worked in factories to supplement the meagre income of their father.

It was this lack of school resources that Foster's Education Act of 1870 was designed to remedy. This divided the country into areas and charged local School Boards with the responsibility of building schools where there were too few, and monitoring the standards of existing schools. The Act was followed by another, in 1880, making attendance compulsory to the age of ten and appointing attendance officers.

The new Board Schools were built and received with evangelical fervour. These red brick monuments to a new age of education had furniture to match. As the North of England School Furnishing Company's 1885 catalogue states, their large locker desks 'being entirely of wood, and being massive and highly finished were suitable for buildings of high character'.

SCHOOL FURNITURE

It was with the growth of Board Schools that such companies either established themselves or saw the chance to expand into a new area. Some companies had started as general office stationers and saw new opportunities, while others simply started afresh, but all had one objective – to make and sell desks and other pieces of school furniture as fast as the new schools demanded them. E.J. Arnold and Son Ltd., Illingworth, Ingham and Company, and George M. Hammer and Company were all businesses who developed a keen interest in the manufacture of School furniture.

The earliest manufactured desks were simple affairs commendable for their durability but certainly not for comfort or ease of use. They often followed designs that had previously been quite literally hammered out in a collaboration between the village blacksmith and local joiner.

One of the most elementary desks was nothing more than a pine bench, perhaps

▼ *The long bench desks which characterized the Victorian schoolroom were also found in French schools, along with the dunce's cap.*

46

▶ *This dual desk of 1900 is sturdily built of cast iron and oak. The desk top is flat, not sloped, with slots for slates, a groove for pens and one central inkwell. Beneath it is a book ledge, backed by a board. The hinged seat could be raised. The iron supports are in Gothic style.*

with a hat shelf beneath, upon which five or so pupils would sit, with a pine plank top supported by a pivoted iron arm at each end, acting as a desk surface. Apart from constant surreptitious fidgetting to sit more comfortably or find an extra inch of space, such desks gave children one other cause for concern. The desk top could be turned over by means of the pivoted arms to become a back rest for the bench instead. One clumsy pupil arriving at, or exiting from, the desk in haste could easily disturb the desk top and thus ruin an hour or so's work in the sand trays that were written in before slates became commonplace.

A step up from the convertible desk/seat was the dual desk. This comprised a bench seat with backrest attached by runners to the end supports or standards of the desk surface. Sometimes the desk top would be angled to facilitate reading and there would be a foot rest running the width of the seat. Again, manufacturers simply modified a basic design, making use of cast, rather than wrought, iron for runners and backrest stays.

Practical and decorative refinements were made to the dual desks as manufacturers fought for orders and strove to stamp their own identity on their products. Book ledges, perhaps faced with a board to prevent books falling off, were fitted and slate slots were cut into the desk's surface. Some tops were also bored out to take inkwells which would be distributed from an inkwell tray.

Drill, or P.E. as it was to become known in later years, was often carried out in the classroom with no thought given to changing clothes for the exercise. Some desk makers capitalized on this by hingeing their desks' seats so that they could be turned up. Once this was done there was, it was claimed, sufficient room for drill actually at the desk.

SINGLE-SEAT DESKS

The move away from desks that sat two or more pupils to single-seat desks took place relatively slowly though received due attention and advertisement from the manufacturers. In 1885, one firmly advocated single-seat desks 'on account of the important educational and sanitary advantages resulting from the isolation of students when engaged in study.' Soon, single-seat locker desks were being produced of a design that would remain familiar to generations of schoolchildren to come.

The hinged desk top concealed a locker section for books and papers and was made of such woods as oak or pine and beech. In general, such desks were attached to seats by iron runners. Only specialist desks, such as art desks or those designed for masters, were freestanding.

Today, relatively few school desks can be found in antique shops. Despite being produced in their thousands, many were discarded en masse or allowed to fall into severe disrepair. If found, however, these simple and appealing industrial products make a charming addition to any child's study area within the home. With a little care and attention, old damaged examples can be successfully restored, and can be made into attractive pieces of furniture.

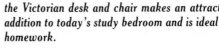

▲ *Stripped and freshly waxed, with its graffiti sanded down and a comfortable cushion added, the Victorian desk and chair makes an attractive addition to today's study bedroom and is ideal for homework.*

DESIGN IN FOCUS
The Glendenning's Patent Desk

THE GLENDENNING'S PATENT ADJUSTABLE IS MADE FROM PINE, BEECH AND IRON. THE SLOPED LOCKER CAN BE MOVED 5 INCHES (12.5CM) TO OR FROM THE SEAT, HAS A HINGED READING LEAF AND FEATURES AN INKWELL COVERED BY A SLIDING BRASS PLATE.

THE CHAIR WAS DESIGNED BY A DR ROTH WITH AN ADJUSTABLE PAD FOR THE SPINE TO FACILITATE CORRECT POSTURE.

SET AT 33½ INCHES (84CM) HIGH AND 36 INCHES (90CM) LONG, THE DESK AND CHAIR HAVE CAST-IRON STANDARDS AND ARE JOINED BY A CAST-IRON RUNNER. THE FOOT RAIL IS FITTED WITH ROLLERS, AND A BRASS TABLET IS INSCRIBED WITH THE NAME OF THE MANUFACTURER — COLMAN & GLENDENNING. LATER MODELS OF THE GLENDENNING'S FEATURED A FOLDING COPY REST, FIXED FOOT BOARDS AND ALSO ALLOWED VERTICAL ADJUSTMENT OF BOTH THE SEAT AND LOCKER.

IN 1883, THE PATENT FOR THE GLENDENNING'S WAS RENEWED WHEN THE NORTH OF ENGLAND SCHOOLS FURNISHING COMPANY GAINED EXCLUSIVE RIGHTS TO ITS MANUFACTURE, ADVERTISING IT IN THEIR 1884 CATALOGUE AT 31/6D.

(1) ADJUSTABLE SPINE PAD

(2) HINGED READING LEAF

(3) HINGED, SLOPING DESK TOP

(4) LOCKER MOVES FORWARD AND BACK

(5) FOOTREST HAS ROLLERS BENEATH IT

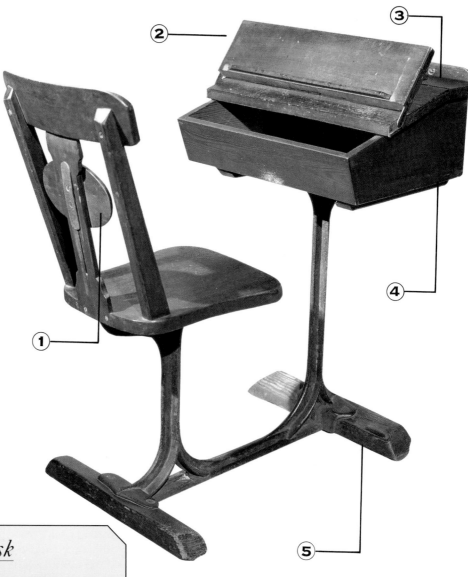

Oak Locker Desk

THIS ROBUST SLOPE-TOP DESK IS JOINED BY RUNNERS TO A CHAIR WITH A TILTING SEAT.

The educational reforms of the 19th century are really responsible for the design of the desks that have seen generations of children through their schooling.

The Great Reform Bill of 1832 extended the franchise to many more men. It was felt that better schooling would help future voters to understand and follow the politics of the country. Progress was slow but the Acts of 1870 and after gradually saw to it that more people were educated.

Neither local joiner and blacksmith or general cabinet-maker could keep up with the increasing demand for desks, so it was quite natural that in this time of growing industrialization companies would establish themselves to satisfy the demand.

The patent for the Glendenning's Adjustable, the 'perfect

·PRICE GUIDE·

School Desks

▼ DESKS TENDED TO BE MADE STRONGLY BUT CHEAPLY, USING SCREWS RATHER THAN CABINETMAKERS' JOINTS.

PRICE GUIDE ❸

▲ A RESTORED DESK WHICH, WITH ITS BACK PANELLING, MAY HAVE BEEN USED BY A TEACHER.

PRICE GUIDE ❸

▲ WROUGHT-IRON LEGS AND HINGES SECURE THIS ORDINARY TURN-OF-THE-CENTURY DESK.

PRICE GUIDE ❸

◀ A CLUMSILY REPAIRED DESK IN ORIGINAL CONDITION, UNITED TO A STICK-BACK CHAIR WITH A SHAPED SADDLE SEAT.

PRICE GUIDE ❹

▶ A VICTORIAN SINGLE-SEAT DESK OF OAK AND WROUGHT IRON. THE DESK HAS A BOOK LEDGE, WITH CURVED CHAIR BACK AND TILTING SEAT.

PRICE GUIDE ❹

instrument of education', was first taken out in 1880. A Dr Liebreich had stated that such ailments as short-sightedness, spinal curvature and flat chests were caused by poorly designed desks and that this model, combined as it was with Dr Roth's chair, would prevent such evils.

The Glendenning's represented a notable advance in its time. Little account, if any, had previously been taken of the disparity in sizes between children, so practically all suffered some discomfort while at work. With its adjustable locker, the Glendenning's gave at least 2½ inches (6.25cm) leeway either side of a central position.

Early desks from most manufacturers were rarely marked with any form of brand or maker's name even though some items of school furniture carried names such as 'Invincible' and 'Imperial' that aptly reflected the tone of the age. However, both the North of England Schools Furnishing Company and E.J. Arnold and Son Ltd took to identifying their products by inscribing the company name on a circular brass tablet between about 1895 and 1910.

Other names to look for include J.W. Bean and Son, McCorquodale and Company and William and Thomas May.

POINTS TO WATCH

■ Check that hinges are secure and not replacements.

■ Make sure that all pivoted parts move freely.

■ Check for woodworm damage – if it is not too extensive it can easily be remedied and repaired. Never take a woodworm infested piece of furniture into your home as the infestation can spread.

■ Check for metal fracture.

Children's Illustrated Books

The advent of colour printing in the 19th century had enormous impact on Victorian children's books. It opened the way for beautiful illustrations, some of which are true works of art

Turning through the pages of a Victorian child's story book, today's readers can still marvel at the sheer quality and vitality of the illustrations that were produced to entice young readers so many years ago. Books were printed for children of all ages and mostly intended to educate as well as entertain. Adventure books, fairy stories as well as colourful alphabet and spelling books blossomed as techniques in colour printing were developed and improved.

Books illustrated by some of the most famous names such as Walter Crane, Randolph Caldecott and Kate Greenaway are today keenly sought-after, but while first editions remain coveted collector's prizes, many subsequent editions are still within the average collector's pocket.

The first books specifically designed for children appeared as long ago as the mid-

COMPARISONS

Hand-colouring

UNTIL THE 1850s, MOST BOOKS WERE COLOURED BY HAND — A LABORIOUS AND COSTLY PROCESS, WHICH MEANT THAT EDITIONS CONTAINING COLOURED PLATES OFTEN COST HALF AS MUCH AGAIN AS UNCOLOURED ONES. THIS MID-19TH CENTURY ILLUSTRATION IS TYPICAL OF HAND-COLOURED WORK.

Lost your mittens! you naughty kittens!
Then you shall have no pie.
　　　Mee-ow, mee-ow, mee-ow.
No, you shall have no pie.
　　　Mee-ow, mee-ow, mee-ow.

17th century. As it became increasingly apparent that children could be encouraged to read if their books, even solid instructional texts, were attractively illustrated, Victorian publishers started to vie with each other for the attention of their young readers. There was also a growing distinction between books intended to instruct and those designed purely for entertainment.

SCHOOLROOM BOOKS

For very young children, alphabet books abounded, some of them based around appealing themes such as zoos, gardens or railways. Attractive early readers and grammars, too, were commonplace and in addition there was an increasing number of titles explaining, with the aid of illustration, the wonders of geology and other sciences to the Victorian child. Purely educational books apart, many lighter Victorian children's books were merely thinly disguised moral tracts. Indeed, until the mid-19th century, books of entertainment, including fairy tales, were regarded as frivolous, even immoral by some.

Victorian strictness and emphasis on behaviour is clearly evident in titles such as *The Fat Cat or do not ask for all you see.* Cautionary tales, too, were commonplace

▼ *Books which were enjoyed by the children of the last century can still give great pleasure today. Those with impressive illustrations or bindings are well worth collecting and there are a variety to choose from.*

◄ *Attractive bindings for children's books continued to be produced well into the 20th century and are surprisingly easy to find. These look good on almost any surface or shelf. They can also be used to add to the period feel of a room.*

forbidding, however. Novelty books had been in existence since the early 19th century. By the 1850s, a variety of 'trick books' had appeared, employing a wealth of ingenious devices, including elaborate, many-tiered, 'pop-up' images with sliding panels and tabs or levers that moved ships across oceans or made Humpty Dumpty fall off his wall.

ILLUSTRATION AS AN ART FORM

As advances in colour printing brought an increasing number of illustrators to the fore, there were three in particular who stood head and shoulders above their contemporaries in their skill and invention. Today, they are regarded as the giants of the field.

Walter Crane was one of the most famous of all children's book illustrators. His distinctive, complex illustrations often required as many as six or eight separate blocks and printings. Sometimes he wrote out the text himself in clear graceful letters and made use of inventive, decorative motifs. His work revolutionized the traditional children's 'toy' books – cheap, paper-covered nursery-rhyme and story books consisting of six or eight square pages of colour illustration.

Randolph Caldecott's style was quite different from Crane's. His strong outlines were full of movement and lively expression, with humorous figures which bordered on caricature. The great trio is completed by Kate Greenaway. After her discovery as a relatively unknown illustrator in 1878, she became one of the most successful, as well as one of the most popular, of Victorian book illustrators. Her beautifully dressed little boys and girls, appear in elegant settings and neat cottage gardens, and her designs were distinctively light and open.

CHILDHOOD CLASSICS

Some titles can be said to have become children's classics and are still read by children the world over, attracting new illustrators through successive generations.

The collection of old folk and fairy tales made by the Brothers Grimm, first published in English in 1823, became what was probably the most popular anthology of its kind ever published. Hans Christian Andersen's collection, first translated into English in 1846 as *Wonderful Stories for Children*, also became universally loved.

Lewis Carroll's *Alice's Adventures in Wonderland* (1865), together with *Through the Looking Glass and What Alice Found There* (1872), has been published in many languages and illustrated by a total of over 100 artists, from the original and much loved woodblock illustrations by Sir John Tenniel to Arthur Rackham in the early 20th century, and, more recently, Salvador Dali.

▼ *The pictorial cloth bindings on some 19th-century children's books are truly stunning. This embossed and gilded design with its naturalistic motifs is typically Victorian.*

and instilled, often in a quite terrifying manner, the consequences of doing wrong. Among the most famous of cautionary tales was, and still is, *Struwwelpeter* (meaning 'slovenly Peter'). Its stories contain a graphic account of a little girl being burnt to death after playing with matches, and a young boy who has his thumbs cut off as a punishment for sucking them. Although *Struwwelpeter* was, in fact, written as a parody of the over-moralistic stories on offer in picture books, it reflects the type of relentless moralizing fed to children in the form of rhymes or stories.

Not all children's books were quite so

Books for Pleasure

Despite the serious undertones of much Victorian children's literature, a good number of books emerged that were free of moralizing or didactic content. The nursery classic, *The Butterfly Ball*, first appeared in 1807 and remained an enduring favourite. Later in the century, and also for the young reader, there was Robert Louis Stevenson's *A Child's Garden of Verses* (1885) of which one stunning edition contained the beautiful Art Nouveau illustrations by Charles Robinson, brother of Heath Robinson.

For older children there were racy adventure stories such as the successful series by R. M. Ballantyne. His *Coral Island: A Tale of the Pacific Ocean* (1858) is perhaps the most famous of his best-sellers for the teenage market. Stevenson is said to have read it as a boy and been inspired to write his classic *Treasure Island* (1883).

Another satisfying area for the collector is that of fairy tales, where stories of dreamy, imaginary worlds gave ample inspiration to illustrators.

▶ *By the 1840s, collections of fairy tales were widely published. Some of the most decorative illustrations and cover designs were inspired by stories of fantasy and magic.*

PRICE GUIDE ❷

▼ *Books illustrated by Kate Greenaway are popular with collectors and first editions can command high prices. Her beautiful images depicting idealized scenes and immaculate children were so successful that her designs were used on a huge range of other products ranging from china to greetings cards and ceramic nursery tiles.*

PRICE GUIDE ❸ ❹

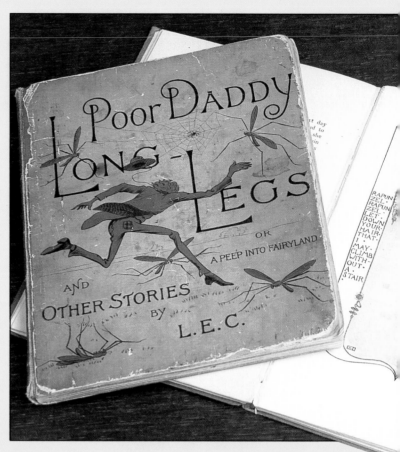

▲ *Lewis Carrol so admired John Tenniel's political cartoons in* Punch *that he approached him to illustrate his* Alice in Wonderland. *About 100 artists have since illustrated* Alice *and there have been countless editions, including this humorous parody, dated 1902.*

PRICE GUIDE ❷

▲ One of the hallmarks of Randolph Caldecott's illustrations was a great sense of fun communicated through lively characters. The Victorians were delighted by his 16 books for children and bought copies in great numbers.

PRICE GUIDE ❶

▶ Adventure stories are collectable for their fine, often colourful, covers designed to attract young 19th century readers. Frequently they were illustrated with lavish colour plates and dramatic frontispieces which served to bring these gripping tales to life.

PRICE GUIDE ❶

PRICE GUIDE

Educational Books

Learning is a central element of all children's reading but some Victorian books were definitely intended for the schoolroom rather than the play room. Even in the stricter days of the last century, attempts were made to make learning fun and today many of these books provide a rich source for the collector.

As well as the 'Three Rs', history, geography and religion could all be made more enticing with the aid of lively illustrations. Among the most important geography books were those by the American writer Samuel Griswold Goodrich (1793-1860) better known by his pseudonym of 'Peter Parley'. His educational books, totalling over a hundred, covered subjects as diverse as shipwrecks and astronomy as well as geography, and were so popular that they were pirated by publishers in Britain.

Rebus books, in which a symbol was used to represent a word or a syllable, such as a picture of an eye for the word 'I', had a long history and were originally used to teach children religion rather than give them an enjoyable puzzle.

▲ For the well-to-do Victorian child, Sunday was set aside for pious reading. Many picture books set out to explain bible stories and prayers in an enjoyable way.

PRICE GUIDE ❷ ❸

▼ Children's magazines began to appear in the late 18th century but well into the 19th century booklets such as *Alfred the Great* had a definite educational purpose.

PRICE GUIDE ❷

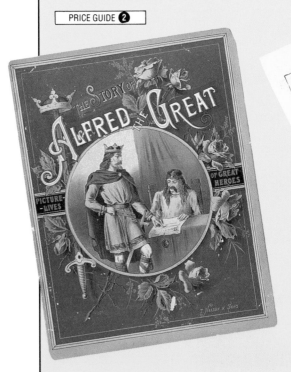

▲ Early alphabet and spelling books make delightful collectables. This story book in words of one syllable shows how, typically, reading and good behaviour were taught simultaneously.

PRICE GUIDE ❷

▶ PRICE GUIDE ◀

▲ *Nursery books, not surprisingly, are hardly ever found in immaculate condition. This amusing* Child's Easy Reading Book *dated 1859 is in a fragile state.*

PRICE GUIDE ❶

◀ *School textbooks were always assured of a large and ready market. Even some of the most turgid tracts had their share of colour illustrations.*

PRICE GUIDE ❷ ❸

◀ COLLECTOR'S TIPS ▶

The more enjoyed a child's book has been during its lifetime, the less likely it is to have survived. If it has, the chances are that it will be rather battered and defaced and of little value to the collector. It is partly for this reason that copies of highly regarded titles in good condition are so rare and so highly priced. Even so, it is still possible to build up a beautiful and enjoyable collection of books by concentrating on less famous titles or, simply, later editions.

FIRST EDITIONS

A first edition includes all copies of a book as it was first printed and published, along with the repeated printings with minor textual alterations. A first edition becomes a second edition only when the text has been reset or the format changed. Not surprisingly, first editions have no printing history in their inside pages but if you are lucky, there will be a date of publication on the title pages. Dating undated books may require careful study of catalogues or specialist books, or the help of an expert.

Limited editions are those including a statement that a certain, limited number of copies have been printed: they are generally numbered and may be signed by the author or illustrator or both, in which case the value would be even higher.

Editions are also published in different bindings: the more impressive, unusual or original the binding, and the better its condition, the greater the value.

CARING FOR BOOKS

However they are arranged, the books should be kept under the right conditions, preferably in glass-fronted book cases. The

Colour Printing

THE DIFFERENCE BETWEEN EARLY AND LATE COLOUR PRINTING CAN BE QUITE STRIKING. AT FIRST IT WAS ONLY POSSIBLE TO REPRODUCE CRUDE TONES BUT LATER, COLOURS BECAME MORE SUBTLE.

Struwwelpeter – a Victorian Favourite

THIS FAMOUS COLLECTION OF CAUTIONARY TALES FIRST APPEARED IN GERMANY IN 1845 AND RAPIDLY BECAME ONE OF THE BEST-SELLING NURSERY BOOKS OF ALL TIME. ITS AUTHOR, HEINRICH HOFFMAN, A MEDICAL DOCTOR IN FRANKFURT, FRUSTRATED BY THE OVER-MORALISTIC STORIES ON OFFER IN PICTURE BOOKS, PRODUCED IT IN AN EXERCISE BOOK TO AMUSE HIS FOUR-YEAR-OLD SON. A YEAR LATER HE WAS PERSUADED TO PUBLISH HIS COLLECTION OF GRUESOME STORIES, SUBTITLED WITH DELIBERATE IRONY: 'PRETTY

STORIES AND FUNNY PICTURES FOR LITTLE CHILDREN.' THE RESULT WAS INSTANT SUCCESS.

THERE FOLLOWED NUMEROUS EDITIONS IN MANY LANGUAGES, INCLUDING ENGLISH. ALTHOUGH ORIGINALLY WRITTEN AS A TYPE OF SPOOF, IN ITSELF IT INSPIRED PARODIES, SUCH AS THE *EGYPTIAN STRUWWELPETER* (1899), CREATED ON BROWN PAPER TO RESEMBLE ANCIENT EGYPTIAN PAPYRUS BY THREE CHILDREN OF A VIENNESE DOCTOR, AGAIN WITHOUT THOUGHT OF SERIOUS PUBLICATION.

① COLOUR OUT OF REGISTER INDICATES HAND-COLOURED ENGRAVING

② MORE REFINED ILLUSTRATION AND BARE FACE DENOTES LATER DATE

③ FLAT AREAS OF COLOUR SUGGEST WOODBLOCK PRINTING METHOD

④ PAGES OF REINFORCED LINEN GAVE ADDED STRENGTH

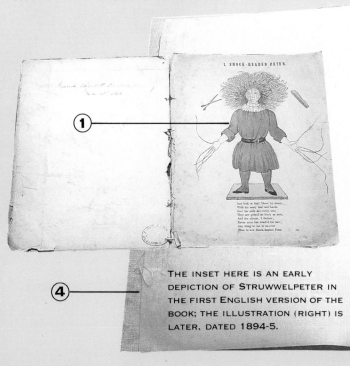

THE INSET HERE IS AN EARLY DEPICTION OF STRUWWELPETER IN THE FIRST ENGLISH VERSION OF THE BOOK; THE ILLUSTRATION (RIGHT) IS LATER, DATED 1894-5.

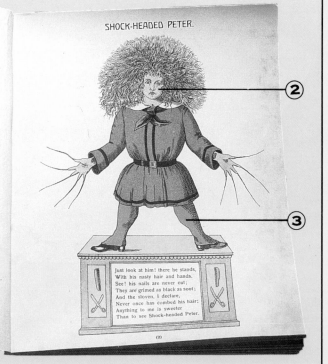

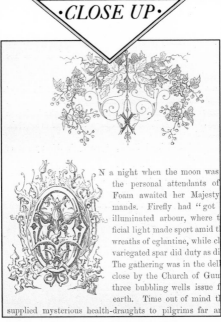

① ORNAMENTAL MAJUSCULE

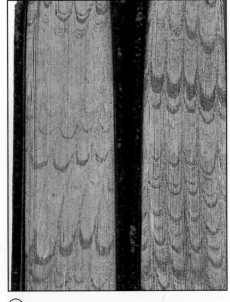

② MARBLED PAGES

③ EMBOSSED BINDING

① LOOK OUT FOR BEAUTIFULLY ENGRAVED INITIAL CAPITAL LETTERS, OFTEN USED TO EMBELLISH CHAPTER OPENINGS.

② DECORATIVE BINDINGS ARE ONE OF THE ATTRACTIONS OF BOOK COLLECTING. THESE PAGES WERE HAND-COLOURED.

③ IMPRESSIVE BINDINGS IN GOOD CONDITION WILL INVARIABLY ENHANCE THE VALUE OF ANTIQUE BOOKS.

④ HANDWRITTEN INSCRIPTIONS CAN HELP TO DATE CERTAIN BOOKS. LOOK OUT FOR AUTHOR-SIGNED EDITIONS.

⑤ PRINTING INFORMATION APPEARS ON INSIDE PAGES. LOOK FOR PUBLISHER'S NAME AND DATE.

⑥ DETAIL FROM AN EARLY CHILD'S READER WITH CLOTH PAGES; IT HAS BEEN COLOURED BY ONE OF ITS OWNERS.

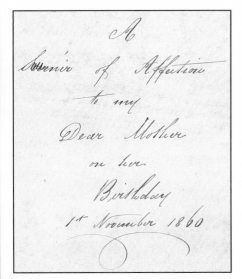

④ PERSONAL INSCRIPTION

⑤ PUBLISHERS AND DATE

⑥ ILLUSTRATION ON CLOTH

correct humidity level is most important and should ideally be between 50 and 65 per cent. Any higher and the glues, pastes, leather, linen and paper of which the books are made will start to rot and attract fungi and destructive insects. If, on the other hand, books are kept in over-dry conditions (for example, too near a radiator) the paper and other materials may become parched and brittle.

Always dust books gently but thoroughly along the tops and edges after you buy them, then keep them dusted. Inspect regularly for insects or any traces of mould. *Foxing* of paper, first appearing as tiny, pinhead-sized, brown or orange spots which are the spores of fungi, is caused by damp conditions. The spots may later turn purple or even black. Keep foxing at bay by interleaving valuable books with a proprietary impregnated paper, allowing one sheet to every eight pages.

POINTS TO WATCH

■ The work of many of the great children's book illustrators and authors was plagiarized in their time, so look closely at an artist's style to ascertain whether material is genuine.

■ Look out for signatures or initials of illustrators in the illustrations themselves: some artists identified themselves by using a particular monogram.

■ Check condition of books carefully before buying, and that pages are complete and in a reasonable state.

▲ *Pop-up books with their appealing, three-dimensional images, were popular in Britain by the 1850s.*

The Magic Lantern

The magic lantern show, with subjects ranging from the serious to the comic, was a highly popular form of entertainment in Victorian drawing rooms

The Victorian insistence on moral purpose meant that the average middle-class family always expected their leisure hours to be occupied, preferably with useful or educational tasks. Thankfully, as far as the younger members were concerned, all was not high sobriety. The magic lantern, an early form of slide projector, provided a form of entertainment that combined not only the scientific and the didactic, but also the melodramatic and the boisterously humorous.

Magic lantern shows were traditional drawing-room entertainment for children's parties and the Christmas season. Either the family would put on their own lantern show or, in the days when the lantern was still an expensive item, an itinerant showman might be asked in to amaze and terrify his audience with such delights as 'Mystify & Co' (an

Magic Lantern Slides

THE COLOURFUL AND FREQUENTLY COMIC SUBJECTS OF MAGIC LANTERN SLIDES MAKE THEM PARTICULARLY APPEALING TO MODERN COLLECTORS.

original fairy tale, illustrated by beautiful hand-painted pictures with rapid changes and illusions).

However, lantern shows were by no means exclusively reserved for the family drawing room. Like the popular giant panoramic views and dioramas, they were also public spectacles, to be seen in church halls or scientific venues such as the celebrated Royal Polytechnic Institution in Regents Park, London, where large, painted $6\frac{1}{2}$in $\times$ $8\frac{1}{2}$in (16cm $\times$ 21cm) glass slides were projected on to an area of 650 square feet (63 square metres).

The idea of illuminating an object from behind so that it cast a shadow on a wall or screen was first developed in the Far East where it attained the status of an art form. Thin, hinged translucent characters were painted with bright colours and ornamented with filigree so that when light was shone through them, they produced colourful projected images.

It was not until the 17th century that Europeans began to investigate such optical possibilities for themselves. Athanasius Kircher was the first to describe methods of projecting images through transparent glass but it was his Dutch contemporary, Christiaen Huygens, who in 1649 illustrated and described the workings of a simple projector. Seven years later Samuel Pepys recorded in his famous diary his purchase of 'a lanthorn with pictures in glasse, to make strange things appear on the wall.' By the end of the century the new instrument had become widely popular.

LANTERN ILLUMINATION

Magic lanterns were fundamentally dependent on the power of their light source. In the early years they relied on daylight, the flame of a candle, or an oil lamp. A concave lens concentrated the light, and potential flickering was reduced by the addition of a chimney, initially made of glass. A paraffin burner introduced by the Newton Lantern company proved popular but the search still continued for stronger and safer light sources. Lime, ignited by a combustible combination of gases, produced the searing brilliance of limelight but was considered a rather dangerous method of illumination, and by the end of the century it had given way to the electric arc lamp.

Different types of lantern were available to suit every purse. The cheapest sold for as little as one shilling but quality was correspondingly poor. The most popular full-size models, which sold for around £1, were made from black tinplate. Enthusiasts of limited means could buy the lenses on their own and construct the casing and build in the light source themselves.

Particularly prized were lanterns made from Russian iron, such as those manufactured by Perken, Son and Company, whose trade name was Optimus. One of their expensive models, boasting mahogany-panelled doors and an elaborate stand, was advertised as being suitable for the drawing room. Similar but slightly less elaborate lanterns with mahogany or walnut cases and brass fittings were made by well-known manufacturers such as Reynolds & Branson, and sold for around £4. The same company also specialized in the so-called 'science lanterns' in which limited practical experiments could take place in the space between lens and light source and be projected on to a screen. A microscope attachment could enlarge very small objects, making the lanterns suitable for specific teaching purposes.

DISSOLVING VIEWS

New techniques were soon developed to produce an illusion of movement. In the 1840s Childe and Hill produced their 'dissolvent views' which involved placing two lanterns side by side and alternately covering and uncovering the lenses so that one scene 'dissolved' into another. The production of the double or biunial lantern towards the end of the century with one lens placed on top of the other eventually led to triunials and even quadrunials – forerunners of the banks of projectors used in today's

▲ *Magic lantern shows were popular entertainment at children's parties and at Christmas time, when those with Biblical subjects were considered highly suitable. This group of children are enjoying a scene of the three Magi being guided by the Star of Bethlehem to pay homage to the newborn Christ.*

Lantern Styles

LATE-VICTORIAN TIN AND BRASS MAGIC LANTERN WITH GAS BURNERS AND TAPS VISIBLE AT THE BACK.

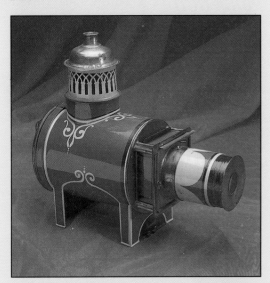

A DECORATIVELY PAINTED TIN AND BRASS LANTERN WITH AN ELABORATE CHIMNEY, FROM THE LAST DECADE OF THE 19TH CENTURY.

BRASS, IRON AND TINPLATE LANTERN FEATURING A PARAFFIN BURNER WITH AN ADJUSTABLE WICK LIKE AN OIL LAMP.

·PRICE GUIDE·

MAGIC LANTERNS AND OPTICAL TOYS

Interest in magic lantern equipment and optical toys has grown enormously in recent years, as people have rediscovered the lantern show as an amusing entertainment and an important precursor of the cinema. Rusty lanterns, zoetropes and praxinoscopes can be picked up cheaply in junk shops, but it is worthwhile going to a specialist dealer for equipment in good working order. Although lanterns were illuminated by candles, gas, paraffin and limelight in the Victorian era, many were subsequently converted to electricity.

▲ *A newspaper advertisement illustrating the biunial, or double lantern. Its two lenses placed one above the other allowed two slides to be precisely aligned so that one picture could dissolve into another. It could also be used to superimpose small images on to larger scenes.*

sophisticated cinemas operating all over the world.

The slides themselves were often quite elaborate. The earliest painted versions were large and came in mahogany frames. By the mid-Victorian period the 3¼in × 3¼in (8cm × 8cm) format, faced with a protective glass cover, had become standard, while the format favoured on the Continent and in the U.S.A. was 4in × 3¼in (10cm × 8cm).

Elegantly hand-painted views gave way in the 1850s to mass-produced slides printed by lithographic transfer and produced in their millions by companies such as Butcher and Son of London. These were generally sold in boxes of eight for two shillings. Comic stories, topical, religious and educational subjects were all favourites.

It was also possible to buy special paints and glass plates for homemade pictorial slides, and to purchase special photosensitized lantern plates for photographic slides. These were often hand-tinted, and were particularly popular with the devotees of the temperance movement who used them to illustrate turgid sentimental and moralistic tales about the evils of drink ('Look not upon the Wine with its Ruby Glow', 'Abstinence and Hard Work' were two such tales.) Shows were spiced up with some hymn singing to words projected on the screen and the odd advertisement for Quaker Oats or Beecham's Powders.

THE ILLUSION OF MOVEMENT

Panoramic slides, often with comic subjects, were perennially popular. When slid along the front of the projector they produced a crude impression of movement, and they inspired the development of an ingenious array of mechanical slides. The simplest system involved moving one slide across another, to create such images as an old woman losing her bonnet

▼ *A turn-of-the-century iron and brass magic lantern specially made for a child. It is in reasonable condition and comes with its wooden box.*

PRICE GUIDE **5**

▼ *A Kromscop from c. 1899. This interesting optical device is a viewer which adds the illusion of colour to any black-and-white slide placed inside by means of three coloured filters.*

PRICE GUIDE **8**

Mechanical Slides

◀ *A classical slide of a man eating rats. The rat is on a circular glass, the man's jaw is on a lever glass.*

PRICE GUIDE **4**

▶ *A relatively simple slide showing a cat being teased with a mouse. The glass lever on the left moves the monkey's hand which dangles the rodent.*

PRICE GUIDE **3**

◀ *A chromotrope with two painted glass discs which counter-rotate to make vivid patterns.*

PRICE GUIDE **2**

and wig in a high wind. Vertical movement was possible with the lever slide, as was a circular rotation of up to 45 degrees. The upper image, coated with lamp black, would be slowly moved, perhaps to reveal a girl whose nose seemed to grow and grow.

OPTICAL TOYS

Rotary movement could be used to depict a windmill in full sail or the classic image of a man in bed whose jaws opened to swallow innumerable rats. Several related optical toys produced different effects, but perhaps the most fascinating was Beale's Choreutoscope of 1866. Based on the theory of persistence of vision, this variety of lantern slide allowed several slightly different images (usually of a dancing skeleton) to be cranked past the small window in the lantern. Each image was seen only for a fraction of a second before the shutter fell, and the next image was projected, giving an illusion of continuous movement. Such was the theory behind many other optical toys, including the Thaumatrope, the Phenakistoscope, the Praxinoscope and the Zoetrope. They were initially produced by scientists, but eventually found their way into Victorian drawing rooms. It only needed Eadweard Muybridge's mastery of timelapse photography to push technical developments to the brink of the era of cinematography. The magic lantern, however, continued to hold its own in the early years of cinema, with film and lantern shows often sharing the same programme. After suffering an eclipse in the wake of the First World War the magic lantern is now enjoying a revival, and competitive, though not excessive, prices are being paid for objects that were not so long ago consigned to the dustbin, while hand-painted slides are bought for their artistic merit.

▼ *A late-19th century French praxinoscope presented in its original box with its picture strips. The images reflected in the rectangular mirrors appear to move when the drum is spun round.*

PRICE GUIDE **7**

▶ *Tin and brass magic lantern with its own metal case. The convoluted chimney is typical of many lime-burning lanterns.*

PRICE GUIDE **5**

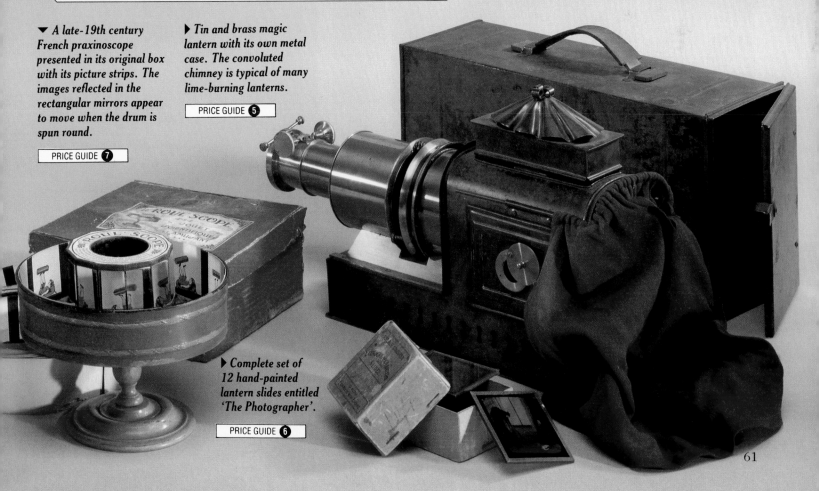

▶ *Complete set of 12 hand-painted lantern slides entitled 'The Photographer'.*

PRICE GUIDE **6**

Teddy Bears

Teddy bears have graduated from being much
hugged childhood toys and have become minor
stars of the auction room, but are still within reach
of most pockets

That most loved of nursery toys, the teddy
bear, made his appearance in the Edwardian
period, and at least part of his success in
Britain was due to that other 'Teddy' who occupied
the throne. By 1910 the bear was the country's most
popular single toy and many people, among them Sir
John Betjeman, went on to treasure this companion
of their childhood throughout their lives.

BEAR BEGINNINGS

The dispute as to whether the teddy originated in
Germany or America has raged for years, though it
now seems more likely that the most significant
commercial production began at the factory of
Margarette Steiff in Geingen-on-Brenz. This small
German manufacturer had begun by producing felt
animals but, after an ambitious nephew, Richard,
joined her in 1897, more interesting lines began.

▼ *The cuddly, passive
nature of bears endeared
them to children from the
start. Bear care is an
essential part of owning a
teddy, and dressing them up
in soldier, sailor or
layman's clothes has long
been a source of fascination
to the young.*

Richard Steiff was particularly interested in the
bear cubs as toys and he sketched and studied them
at Stuttgart Zoo. He was soon aware that a fully
articulated toy was necessary in order to capture the
lively movements of the animal. The prototypes,
made in 1902, were the first of Steiff's products to
have moving limbs. The initial consignments were
sent to America and Britain in 1903, though other
factories were quick to imitate such a concept.

An American called Morris Michtom, founder
of the Ideal Toy Corporation, produced some toy

▲ President Teddy Roosevelt was happy to lend his name to a toy that had so captured the public's affection, and found it, indeed, an asset for publicity purposes.

border dispute between Mississippi and Louisiana in November 1902, when Teddy Roosevelt actually drew a line between the states. It was Michtom who wrote to Roosevelt asking permission to use the name 'Teddy' for the bear.

By 1904 teddy bears from Britain, America and Germany were competing in the international toy market, though the products bore little resemblance to the big-eared, chubby fellows that Berryman had drawn. These first bears are characterized by their long arms and exaggerated but naturalistic back humps. With long, pointed noses and glass or shoe-button eyes, they were created in soft mohair, with pads of leather, leathercloth, felt or plush. Claws, nose and mouth were embroidered in black.

The popularity of the first Steiff bears, shown at the Leipzig Fair in 1903, was such that the firm was soon unable to meet trade demands. By 1907, the peak of the Bärenjåhre (The Bear Years), Steiff's production had risen to 974,000. The fashion declined a little in the years before the First World War, remaining stable until the recent bear boom.

BRITISH BEARS

Steiff bears were somewhat thin and elongated, but those produced in Britain were, in general, much plumper. Kapok, woodwool, cork granules, straw, and sawdust were all used for filling. Two of the materials were sometimes used in the same animal, as straw, for instance, was good for holding the shape of the long nose. The best mohair was obtained from Britain and was always fairly expensive, though cheaper substitutes were soon used. Though golden

bears around 1902, but no attributable early examples are known. However, Michtom was responsible for pinning the name 'Teddy' to the bear as a result of an incident involving American President Theodore Roosevelt, known as 'Teddy'. In 1902 he went bear hunting in Mississippi. When faced with a tiny cub, he refused to shoot. This incident was made famous in a cartoon drawn by Clifford Berryman for the *Washington Post*, which bore the caption 'Drawing the line at Mississippi'. The cartoon referred, in fact, to the settlement of a

▲ *Edwardian bears come in all shapes and sizes from very small ones of a few inches high to those of several feet. Features are often more detailed than on the contemporary bear. Pads are made real with black stitching for claws, and fur is clipped to imitate live bears.*

children's teddy-bear plates, mugs and tea sets were all produced. Puppets, musical boxes, Christmas-tree decorations and gift boxes were part of the teddy-bear cult, while the animal itself could be purchased in all sizes, from a mere couple of inches to display pieces of several feet. For the fashion-conscious little girl, there were mohair muffs with a teddy on the front, while her smart elder sister was happy to be seen promenading with her escort and carrying her teddy-bear mascot. Teddies also appeared on dozens of postcards and in picture books, while the baby was given silver rattles and teethers in his image.

Many children dressed their teddy bears as soldiers and sailors, as military toys were very popular, and some of the well-made uniforms were obviously sewn by mother or nurse. In 1910, one company attempted to launch a female bear, Barbara, made of white mohair, but she was never a great success. In the same year, in Paris, Decamps introduced a tumbling version with a simple motor that was activated by turning the bear's arms, while in Germany a few bear dolls were made, by sewing a bisque doll's face to the back of a conventional teddy head. Any unusual versions, such as those mounted on roller skates, are highly collectable, but it was the original fluffy, warm and cuddly bears which were the loved and treasured companions of the Edwardian child and, indeed, the child of today.

BEAR CARE

Looking after antique bears requires careful attention. It is not advisable to wash or spray Edwardian teddies and any that are extremely dirty should be given to professional restorers. Replacement cardboard joints, wired glass eyes and 'growlers' can also be supplied by experts. Missing limbs are more of a problem to replace as mohair is very difficult to match. It is often easier to make a replacement arm or leg as close to the original as possible, then to hide it with a home-sewn jacket or pair of trousers. Examine bears that are left out as decorative items regularly for moth damage. If kept in a display cabinet, protect them with repellents.

▲ *Pointed noses distinguish the earliest teddy bears from later versions, as, initially, imitation of the real animal was adhered to more strictly.*

bears were always the most popular, there were other coloured versions in cinnamon, black, dark-brown and even red.

Though many bears were made in Britain for such shops as Hamleys, few are attributable, as they were not marked. One of the largest makers was William J Terry, while another manufacturer in London, the Bear Pit, also struggled to keep up with demand. In 1909, Peak Frean introduced their Teddy Bear Nursery biscuits, which remained popular for over half a century, promoted by a group of foot-high bears made by Ralph Dunn & Co. of the Barbican.

THE TEDDY BEAR CULT

During the Edwardian period, the range of bears was greatly increased as new manufacturers of novelty items joined the soft toy makers. Nursery candleholders in the form of seated teddies and

·PRICE GUIDE· ⟩ EDWARDIAN TEDDY BEARS

Exceptionally fine, expensive teddy bears are not difficult to recognize, and it is those in the middle of the range that cause the valuer some thought. Steiff examples, with the classic 'button in the ear', are invariably the most desirable, bears over 28 inches high and in very good general condition selling for between £1,000 and £4,000. The record price for an early Steiff in mint condition was £55,000 paid in June 1986.

Fortunately, most bears still sell at prices between £50 and £250, as examples from all periods are collectable. Particularly desirable are those with makers' names still attached

or with some unusual feature, such as a turning head or mechanical movements. Bears with a growler, which sounds when the teddy is tipped backwards date from 1908. These are particularly desirable. A cheaper press squeaker replaced this. An unusual colour, such as black or red, can also arouse more interest.

The earliest bears – those from the Edwardian period – are most sought-after, even in the smaller sizes. These can be recognized by their more pointed snouts, whereas later bears have snubbed noses and are generally chubbier. Post-1925 bears are more reasonably priced.

The Edwardian Nursery

Presided over by Nanny, the Edwardian nursery with its majestic
rocking horse and delightful toys was the centre of the child's world

The toys and games found in the Edwardian nursery would delight the most sophisticated child today. The room's simple furnishings fade into insignificance against the magnificent rocking horses and finely detailed dolls' houses enjoyed by privileged children at the turn of the century. Toy cupboards overflowed with smaller playthings of all sorts from traditional tops, whips and hoops to the latest in mechanical toys. Exquisite porcelain dolls, which today sit beneath glass cases in museums were once someone's much-loved treasure.

The Edwardian nursery is not difficult to recreate nowadays, although many of the original playthings available have become too precious to entrust to children. Reproductions and modern versions of traditional toys and books are easy to find, along with simple furnishings suitable for children today. Fabrics and wallcoverings depicting nursery-rhyme scenes or Kate Greenaway characters, now readily available, help in evoking the Edwardian scene.

Often situated at the top of the house in the attic, the Edwardian nursery was simply and cleanly furnished, and had a more relaxed atmosphere than that of the previous era.

▼ *Antique furniture and lace add a mellow timelessness to today's nurseries which is impossible to achieve with modern equivalents. However, old coverlets and gowns need careful laundering and are best reserved for special occasions such as christenings.*

▼ *The nursery cupboards contained more toys than ever before and many, like the spinning top, continue to amuse children today.*

The Edwardian nursery was characterized by a new sense of freedom, yet was comfortably secure. Situated at the top of several flights of stairs, its noises muffled by a solid wooden door, the nursery was still a separate world, ruled over by nanny. This was the golden age of childhood, as new clothes, games, travel and education were introduced while, at the same time, there was protection from the day to day problems of life. Few children of the period ever heard their parents quarrel, they were unaware of financial crises and protected from any unpleasant reality that might upset them. Their parents, too, aware of some of the horrors of their own Victorian childhood, tried to make sure that their offspring's infancy and early years were pleasant, safe and healthy. Providing a kind and reliable nanny was employed, their children enjoyed an almost idyllic existence.

NURSERY LIFE

In the large terraced houses of the Edwardian middle class, the nursery was generally situated at the top of the house in the attic. The light, painted room was simply and cleanly furnished, often with old furniture no longer fashionable enough for the lower floors of the house. The large sash windows which looked onto the leafy gardens or terraced street were fitted with bars for safety, yet there was none of the 'prison-like' atmosphere which pervaded the Victorian nurseries of the past.

In the centre of the room there was, invariably, a large strong table, relegated from one of the grander

rooms in the house, covered with a dark-green or red deep-pile cloth with fringed edges. This table was used for meals, lessons, games and painting, while the dark area beneath made an excellent hideaway. A chest of drawers and a toy cupboard were often the only storage furniture in the nursery as most of the available space was taken up with the large toys and playthings popular in the era. The beds, including nanny's, were situated in the night nursery next door.

The coal or gas fire was kept alight on all but the hottest days, as the top of the railed guard was used for airing the babies' clothes and the older children's underwear. On the mantelpiece sat a collection of souvenirs brought back from seaside visits, along with knick-knacks and small gifts that nanny received each Christmas from her charges. Throughout the day, nanny was busy, sewing and knitting in her big wicker armchair and nursing baby in a rocking chair near the fire. As soon as the child could sit up, he was put in a high chair for his meals, a convenient device that often contained a chamber pot to facilitate toilet training, which began at a few months.

Much of the nanny's time was spent washing, dressing and undressing the children, and this arduous task was made worse by the sheer volume of clothes considered proper for a baby. The binder, flannel petticoat, petticoat, gown, jacket, bib, napkin and booties worn every day were all frilled, tucked and embroidered and all had to be washed and meticulously ironed by hand.

Though specially designed furniture was rarely seen in Edwardian nurseries, many parents bought the attractive friezes they saw advertised in magazines and chose curtain fabrics with nursery-rhyme motifs. Popular too were the special nursery tea sets decorated with teddy bears and golliwogs, and nightlight holders in the form of amusing animal heads. A few very fortunate children even ate with cutlery decorated with nursery-rhyme characters, off tablecloths that were especially made for their pleasure.

After dark, in the 19th century, all the nursery games had to be played on the table under the oil lamp. The almost universal use of gas light in suburban houses in the early 20th century meant that all parts of the room could be used and while a steam or electric train ran around the table, another child could play with a dolls' house in a corner or perform a dramatic play in the toy theatre.

TOYS AND GAMES

For the toy collector, the years just before the First World War are known as the Golden Age. Never before had children been offered such a wide range of

▲ *No nursery was complete without a rocking horse on which an Edwardian child could play for hours, pretending to be a dragon-slaying knight, a princess or a highwayman.*

A Change in Fashion

▶ VARIATIONS ON THE POPULAR BUSTER BROWN SUIT WERE HAPPILY WORN BY SMALL BOYS, WHOSE PROGRESSIVE PARENTS HEEDED THE ADVICE OF HYGIENISTS AND TEACHERS, ENCOURAGING FRESH AIR AND FREEDOM.

▼ LITTLE GIRLS WERE ATTRACTIVELY DRESSED IN LOOSE, FLOWING SMOCKS WHICH ALLOWED GREATER FREEDOM OF MOVEMENT THAN EVER BEFORE.

▲ TRADITIONAL SAILOR SUITS WERE STILL WORN AS EVERYDAY DRESS BY EDWARDIAN CHILDREN.

THE FIRST FEW YEARS OF THE 20TH CENTURY SAW A CHANGE IN THE STYLE OF CHILDREN'S CLOTHING FROM STIFF FORMAL LAYERS TO LESS RESTRICTIVE STYLE.

THE VICTORIAN FASHION FOR DRESSING SMALL BOYS IN SKIRTS UP UNTIL THE AGE OF FIVE WAS CHANGED AT THE TURN OF THE CENTURY IN FAVOUR OF SHORT TROUSERS, PARTLY INFLUENCED BY SCHOOL UNIFORMS, SUCH AS THOSE WORN AT ETON.

FURTHER INFLUENCES CAME LATER FROM AMERICA, WHEN IN 1908 A SUNDAY NEWSPAPER FEATURED A COMIC STRIP WITH A CHARACTER CALLED BUSTER BROWN. BUSTER BROWN'S DISTINCTIVE STYLE OF DRESS WAS COPIED BY THOUSANDS, AND A GENERATION OF SMALL BOYS COULD ALL BE SEEN WEARING KNEE-

LENGTH BLOOMERS, A DOUBLE-BREASTED BELTED JACKET AND A WHITE COLLAR WITH BLACK BOW, TOPPED WITH A STRAW BOATER.

FOR GIRLS, THE LIBERTY BODICE — INTRODUCED IN 1908 — SIGNIFIED THE END OF YEARS OF DISCOMFORT. CREATED BY AN OLD, ESTABLISHED CORSET COMPANY, THE BODICE WAS MADE FROM FINELY-KNITTED COTTON STOCKINETTE AND STIFFENED BY BANDS OF TAPE. SOFT SMOCKS WERE EASILY WORN OVER THE TOP OF THE BODICE.

The Daily Routine

THE CHILDREN WOKE EARLY IN THE MORNING TO THE SOUND OF THE FIREGRATE BEING CLEANED BY THE MAID IN THE NEXT ROOM. NANNY, WHO SLEPT IN THE NIGHT NURSERY WITH THE CHILDREN, WAS QUICKLY UP AND DRESSED, READY TO WASH THEM IN THE TIN BATH. BREAKFAST WAS SENT UP FROM THE KITCHEN THEN THE CHILDREN WERE TAKEN DOWN FOR PRAYERS.

DURING THE MORNING THERE WERE SIMPLE LESSONS SET BY NANNY OR OCCASIONALLY BY A VISITING TEACHER. LUNCH WAS USUALLY EATEN IN THE NURSERY, THOUGH IN MORE PROGRESSIVE HOMES THE CHILDREN ATE AT THEIR OWN TABLE IN THE DINING ROOM.

AFTER A SHORT SLEEP IN THE AFTERNOON, FOLLOWED BY A WALK IN THE PARK THE CHILDREN WERE WASHED AND CHANGED AND THEN MARCHED TO THE DRAWING ROOM FOR THEIR HOUR WITH MAMA. HERE THEY LOOKED AT PHOTOGRAPH ALBUMS, TALKED POLITELY, SANG OR RECITED TO VISITORS OR LISTENED TO MUSIC BEFORE RETURNING TO THE NURSERY FOR A LIGHT TEA AND A SHORT PERIOD OF PLAY WITH THEIR TOYS. THEN THEY WERE WASHED AND PUT TO BED.

◀ AFTER BREAKFAST IN THE NURSERY, THE WASHED AND NEATLY-DRESSED CHILDREN WERE TAKEN DOWNSTAIRS FOR MORNING PRAYERS. THEIR BEHAVIOUR IN PUBLIC WAS VERY MUCH NANNY'S RESPONSIBILITY, AND ANY MISCONDUCT BY HER CHARGES IN FRONT OF THE REST OF THE HOUSEHOLD MEANT A SEVERE REPRIMAND.

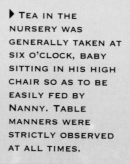

▲ AN AFTERNOON WALK IN THE PARK GAVE THE CHILDREN THEIR DAILY DOSE OF FRESH AIR.

▶ WELL-BROUGHT UP CHILDREN SPENT AN HOUR OR SO WITH MAMA READING, OR WALKING IN THE GARDEN.

▶ TEA IN THE NURSERY WAS GENERALLY TAKEN AT SIX O'CLOCK, BABY SITTING IN HIS HIGH CHAIR SO AS TO BE EASILY FED BY NANNY. TABLE MANNERS WERE STRICTLY OBSERVED AT ALL TIMES.

well-made and attractive playthings. From France, Germany, Japan and America, exciting toys poured into Britain, augmented by finely-made wooden dolls' houses, wax dolls and toy horses, all made in England.

The most prolific maker of large 'strong toys' was G&J Lines, whose goods were sold, in particular, by Gamages, the big London department store. By 1913 Lines were selling miniature Pickford lorries with packing cases, milk floats with churns, farm carts with sacks of produce, railway vans and almost anything that was horse-drawn. Their push-along vendors' carts were excellent toys and the child could pretend to be a baker, confectioner or postman. Lines rocking horses, built on safety rockers, were well made, with beech legs for added strength. These horses were attractively decorated with real manes, tails and miniature saddles.

LIFE IN MINIATURE

Though the majestic rocking horse lorded the nursery, it was when playing with the dolls' house that children re-enacted their own lives. Lines dolls' houses, like the horses, were well designed and strongly made and have survived in some number. Most Edwardian dolls' houses seem to reflect urban life and were made as detached town houses, some with the exciting addition of a bathroom. Though the house, with its painted or lithographed paper façade might be English, its furnishings were almost invariably German and frequently retrospective. From the Sonneberg region came thousands of charming wooden sofas, upholstered in silk or satin, lace-hung beds, chiffoniers, china cabinets and whatnots. Though some Art Nouveau-style furniture in paler woods was made, most dolls' houses resembled homes of the previous decade in their furnishings. Most of the china miniatures, coffee, tea and toilet sets, dessert dishes and kitchen jars also came from Germany, though a few British factories, such as Spode and Wedgwood, still produced some toy sets. For enterprising children, publications were full of ideas for furnishing dolls' houses. Arthur Mee's famous *Children's Encyclopedia* gave instructions for children to make their own dolls' house furniture, and so too did the early children's comics. Activities such as these kept even the most boisterous children quiet.

Two important characters occupied the toy cupboard: the teddy bear and the golliwog. Though the golliwog first appeared as a character in the children's books written by Florence Upton, published in 1895, he was not made in commercial quantities until after 1900, the early models recognizable by their flat noses. He soon became a much loved figure, seen in contemporary illustrations playing the naughty boy. The teddy, standing on hind legs, and with rather doll-like arms, first appeared in 1902, tradition connecting his name with that of Teddy Roosevelt. The first major manufacturer of bears was Margarette Steiff whose products can be recognized by the metal button that was fixed as a trade mark to their ears. Copies of the German product were made in Britain and America, part of its popularity due to the King of England, whose nickname was 'Teddy'. During the period, the bear was seen on nursery china and furniture and was even carried as a mascot by adults.

▶ Choosing the cradle was an exciting task for all expectant mothers. The most popular style was the cast-iron basket type. This was adorned with frills and flounces of muslin and lace – a perfect setting in which to show off the new-born treasure.

While soft toys were loved by boys and girls, as were theatres and puppet shows, the doll was essentially the preserve of females. Before the First World War, the finest French and German bisque dolls were all at the peak of production, many factories producing the 'character' heads with expressive faces that imitated real children, laughing, crying and pouting, rather than the idealized versions so loved by the Victorians. Alongside these traditional wax-and-china-headed dolls there were more adventurous substances such as celluloid suggesting the trends of the future.

Children's Chairs

From the many miniature adult styles to the more functional high-chair designs, the special chairs for small children were some of the most charming additions to the nursery

The Edwardian nursery, generally speaking, was not a place for furnishings of any particular quality. Pieces of furniture judged to be no longer presentable in the formal reception rooms downstairs would soon find their way into the nursery, particularly for use by the nanny. The children, however, were usually provided with their very own small-sized table and chairs, bought specially to suit their needs. Many of these were delightful miniatures of adult styles, but there were also functional, adjustable high chairs made to modern designs.

DURABLE DESIGNS

From as early as the 16th century there are references to special chairs made for children. From the end of the 17th century some of these were in upholstered styles but among the finest chairs that have survived are those in superbly carved walnut. Walnut is susceptible to woodworm but the hard use and constant cleaning which children's chairs underwent has helped to preserve some excellent examples. In the poorer households, there were simple children's chairs, probably of scrubbed oak or beechwood. These durable hardwoods have lasted well and there are many surviving examples. A lot of children's chairs were made in plain, turned pine with rush seats. This traditional pattern was popular from the late 17th century onwards.

A good number of country-style chairs have survived from the 19th century, some of which show the same quality features as the adult versions. The best Windsor types with curved arms and crinoline-type stretchers were made of turned elm, yew or even fruitwood. These designs proved so endlessly popular that they continued to be made up until the First World War and are still being reproduced today. Plain elm and pine chairs were cheaper to produce and a great number were made in the Victorian period for everyday use, some also having a chamber pot in the seat. Rockers with bobbin turning and carpet or leather seats mirrored those used by adults, while a grandfather-style elm armchair might also have been copied for the toddler.

Much more expensive were the fine Mendlesham shapes with the characteristic row of bobbin turning, either in cherry or beech wood, with seats of elm. Cheaper bentwood furniture was mainly imported from Austria and complete suites, including two-seater sofas and tables, were available. The most interesting chairs are those with a musical box concealed under the seat, which

was set up so that it would begin to play as soon as the child sat down.

NOVELTY CHAIRS

It was not unusual for children's chairs to incorporate such a novelty element. Other continental chairs had bells or rattles attached for the baby to play with. In addition to the popular rocking chairs, certain Victorian chairs were made with a bouncing seat. One design made in the 1860s was of mahogany with a curved cane back, fixed to a heavily turned and ornamented stand that incorpo-

◀ *Nursery chairs, whether antique or reproduction, are still in vogue in today's well-appointed children's bedroom.*

▲ *A group of children's chairs from the nursery floor of Osborne House where they were used by Queen Victoria's children. The chairs themselves are in a variety of styles, with vibrant embroidery in striking designs.*

◀ *Children's chairs were frequently made in adult styles. The size of these chairs is indicated by the height of the bed behind.*

▶ *A scaled-down dining table and chairs used by the young Prince of Wales (later Edward VII) and the other royal children at Osborne House.*

high-backed chairs, in similar style, with shell carving on the front of the seat, which were possibly used with special low tables for children to sit at when reading or eating.

HIGH CHAIRS

Chairs on stands – the forerunners of mechanical high chairs – were a late 18th century invention. These dual-purpose chairs featured a child's armchair on a table-like stand so that the infant could be raised to dining table level. The chair could be unbolted from its stand and placed on the floor, where the child could play at the low table. Whether used as a high chair or a play chair, the child was usually restrained by a bar between the arm-rests; occasionally there was also a foot-rest attached to the chair's legs. Chairs of this type, made before 1850, have survived in some number, the most common being the bergère type which had brass bolts fixing the two sections together. Designs frequently displayed the robust lines of adult fashions, using quality woods such as mahogany, made comfortable with plush upholstered seats.

In the Victorian period, a large number

rated a spring device. An adult set this bouncing chair in motion by using a special handle. This style continued to be adapted and improved upon.

EDWARDIAN FASHIONS

As children were made more welcome in the drawing room, it became popular to buy decorative chairs especially for their use. In the Edwardian period, many fashionable ladies even collected antique examples which they arranged in groups. Some of the finest examples dated from the 18th century. Replicas of adult styles, for instance, were the oak 'Country Chippendale', also the superb walnut armchairs with carved shell motifs on the cabriole legs and the centre back. There were

of well-made, upholstered children's chairs in imitation of adult styles were commercially produced. There were button-backed velvet armchairs with cabriole legs, as well as ornately carved, wooden-backed chairs with padded seats. Many were made by skilled cabinetmakers. It was not unusual for a craftsman to make a special chair for a daughter or grandchild which was passed down in the family but rarely used.

The High Chair

THE MECHANICAL HIGH CHAIR FIRST APPEARED IN THE LATE 19TH CENTURY AND BECAME WIDELY USED IN EDWARDIAN TIMES, REMAINING IN PRODUCTION UNTIL AFTER THE FIRST WORLD WAR. THESE ADJUSTABLE CHAIRS COULD BE SET IN SEVERAL DIFFERENT POSITIONS, EITHER HIGH OR LOW OR AS A 'ROCKER'. WITH THE TRAY IN THE BACK POSITION, THE CHILD COULD EAT OR PLAY AT AN ADULT TABLE AND SOME CHAIRS HAVE AN ADDITIONAL LEATHER STRAP FOR EXTRA SAFETY. AS THE TRAY HAD TO BE IN A LIFTED POSITION BEFORE THE CHAIR COULD BE FOLDED, THE CHILD COULD NOT COLLAPSE IT.

THIS TYPE OF CHAIR WAS MADE IN A VARIETY OF STYLES. THE ROCKERS WERE SOMETIMES FRETTED OR MACHINE CARVED, WHILE THE BACKS HAD EITHER WOODEN RAILS, SPINDLES OR, IN SOME CASES, EVEN BUTTONED UPHOLSTERY.

A TYPICAL EDWARDIAN CHAIR WOULD BE MADE OF BEECH OR BIRCH, SOLD EITHER PAINTED WHITE OR STAINED, ACCORDING TO THE FASHION OF THE TIMES.

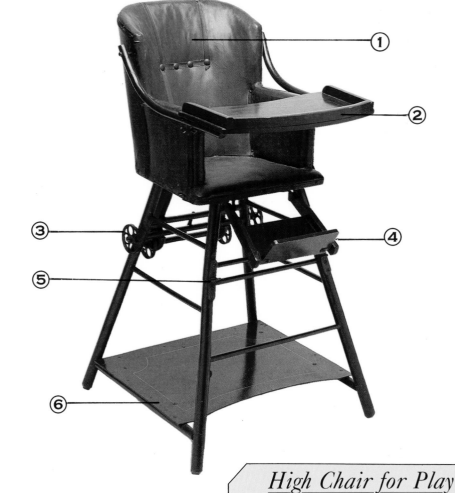

(1) LEATHER UPHOLSTERY WAS EASY TO WIPE CLEAN BUT STAINED READILY.

(2) THE CHAIRS COULD NOT BE UNLOCKED UNLESS THE TRAY WAS FOLDED BACK.

(3) WHEELS FOR MOVING THE CHAIR WHEN IT WAS FOLDED DOWN.

(4) ADJUSTABLE FOOTREST ON A RATCHET, FOR GREATER COMFORT.

(5) HINGES ON FRONT LEGS WERE ORIGINALLY MADE OF CAST IRON.

(6) BOTTOM SHELF BECAME A TABLE WHEN THE CHAIR WAS FOLDED DOWN.

Early High Chair

REGENCY CHILD'S CHAIR BOLTED TO A TABLE-LIKE STAND. THE CHAIR HAS A RESTRAINING BAR AND FOOT-REST.

High Chair for Play

THE LOWER SHELF BECOMES A TABLE, OFTEN WITH BEADS AND A PAINTED PICTURE.

High chairs have been made since at least the 17th century, and were designed not only for toddlers but also for older children so that they could eat at their parents' table. Regency high chairs with their cane seats, plain back rails and footrests were among the most practical ever designed. The child was protected from falling forwards by a cross bar which fixed into the ends of the armrests, a device which was used in a great number of chair styles throughout the 19th century.

HIGH CHAIR DESIGNS

A wide range of bentwood, cane-seated and country-style high chairs were made during the Victorian era. Most were scaled-down versions of adult designs but had extra-long legs. Many Windsor types evolved, becoming simpler after 1900, though still as solidly built.

By the Edwardian era, a large selection of high-chair designs were on offer, made to suit all pockets. The fashion for

▲ A LATE VICTORIAN OR EARLY EDWARDIAN PAINTED MECHANICAL HIGH CHAIR.

PRICE GUIDE ❹

▲ A LATE 19TH CENTURY BECK'S CHAIR MADE IN THE SMOKER'S BOW STYLE.

PRICE GUIDE ❹

◀ AN ELEGANT FRENCH FRUITWOOD HIGH CHAIR WITH CANE SEAT AND BACK.

PRICE GUIDE ❺

▲ AN EDWARDIAN BAMBOO CHAIR WITH ART NOUVEAU AND ORIENTAL TOUCHES.

PRICE GUIDE ❸

▲ AN EBONIZED CHILD'S CHAIR WITH A RUSH SEAT AND A SPINDLE BACK.

PRICE GUIDE ❸

▲ A HARDWOOD, VARNISHED CHAIR IN THE EVER-POPULAR WINDSOR DESIGN.

PRICE GUIDE ❺

▲ AN EDWARDIAN BENTWOOD CHAIR, PROBABLY OF BIRCH, WITH AN ENGRAVED SEAT.

PRICE GUIDE ❸

reproductions meant that many of the old styles continued to be made, while an increasing trend towards 'art in the nursery' led to some progressive designs around the turn of the century. M. H. Baillie Scott, for instance, produced an easy-to-clean, flat-backed chair with a plain fabric-strip seat.

Other Arts and Crafts designers were inspired by the rudimentary simplicity of earlier chairs. In the late 19th century, the William Morris Company made high-backed, cane-seated chairs which closely resembled the so called 'deportment' chairs designed by Sir Astley Paston Cooper (1768-1841), an emi-

nent surgeon who hoped to straighten children's backs by forcing them to sit in a bolt upright position.

POINTS TO WATCH

Fake children's chairs are rare but reproduction Georgian styles are common. When buying an Edwardian mechanical high

chair, check the following details.
■ Wheels should be cast iron.
■ Seats were never upholstered but many have been refurbished to cover up a missing chamber pot: check under the seat.
■ Footrests and trays are often missing or have been replaced.

Mechanical Toys

Inventive and well-crafted mechanical toys delighted children in the
Edwardian nursery and reflected technological advances in the adult
world, as cars, trains and planes were developed

The fortunate child of the Edwardian period was born into the golden age of toys. Increased sophistication in manufacturing techniques, combined with the introduction of mass production, meant that for the first time toys could be produced sufficiently cheaply for the nurseries of all households.

GERMANY LEADS THE FIELD

Because of relatively high labour costs in Britain, most toy production of the mid-19th century was centred in Germany, with some competition from France. In Germany the toy industry was concentrated mainly in the Sonneberg region, where porcelain and wooden toys were made, and at Nuremberg, where there was a heavy specialization in metalwork.

The three most important German makers were Gebrüder Bing of Nuremberg, which was founded in about 1863, Geb-

rüder Marklin, which was started in Göppingen in 1859, and the firm of Ernst Paul Lehmann, which operated in its own idiosyncratic style from Berlin.

The work of Bing is characterized by its solidity and attention to detail. The best of its cars were hand-painted, and had opening doors, and windows with bevelled glass. The toy ships were very heavily con-

structed, with powerful, long-running motors, and could perform complicated manoeuvres. Lithography, where the design was engraved on wood or stone before being printed on tinplate sheets, was used for some of the detail, but much use was also made of hand-painting, both by Bing and its major competitor, Marklin.

The Göppingen firm made a very wide

Handmade Automata

AN EARLY EXAMPLE OF A FRENCH
AUTOMATON DOLL. PARIS WAS NOTED
FOR ITS BEAUTIFUL HANDMADE DOLLS
AROUND THE 1880S, BEFORE THE AGE
OF MASS PRODUCTION. FINE DETAILS,
SUCH AS THE PAINTED PLASTER HEAD
AND EXQUISITE FABRIC OF THE DRESS,
MADE IT A SUPERIOR PIECE.

range of toys, but it is their model transport that is most sought-after now. Again the toys are notably solid in construction, with great emphasis on decorative detail. Like all the major manufacturers, Marklin produced largely for the export market, and model trains were frequently manufactured in the styles and liveries of the importing countries. Likewise, the names and inscriptions on ships were changed according to the requirements of the intended buyer.

By contrast, Lehmann's toys were flimsily built and intentionally frivolous. Even the names express humour. 'Tut-Tut', for instance, is a car driven erratically by a driver who is blowing a hunting horn. Always cheap, these toys were decorated with colourful lithography, and parts were joined with tabs, rather than soldered. The insubstantial motors had cheap, pressed

▶ *A visit to the toyshop was an Edwardian child's delight. The ultimate pleasure was a trip to Hamleys, much as it is today. An increasing number of clockwork toys at the cheaper end of the market were produced to satisfy growing demand. The more expensively made German models were prized possessions, and are a collector's pride today.*

◀ *Edwardian toys became more and more exciting as time went on. Among the traditional building bricks, skittles and soft toys were ever more inventive clockwork creations. Early examples were limited to animals and figures, but as cars and aeroplanes were invented, so they were reproduced in tinplate replicas.*

tinplate gears and spiral rather than coil springs. Their attractive appearance and reasonable price made these toys particularly appealing to the mass market.

COMICAL FIGURES FROM FRANCE

Most notable among the French makers were Fernand Martin, who started his factory in 1878, and Charles Rossignol, who started up in 1868, both firms operating from Paris. Their products were generally more insubstantial than those of the Germans, yet are striking in appearance and often amusing.

Martin specialized in making comical figures of people, frequently satirizing Parisian society. An unusual feature was that his toys were often dressed in fabrics, making them more realistic. Like Lehmann, Martin believed in toys having movements that were amusing in their own right. Martin's range included a drunkard attempting to retain his balance, servants juggling with piles of plates and lawyers arguing their cases.

Much of the work of Rossignol was also ephemeral and cheap. Although some trains were made, they were 'floor runners', and

frequently in very small scale. The company is said to have made the first toy car, even before the Germans, and in 1905 produced a model of the Renault taxi.

The export market was less important to the French than it was to the Germans, and as a result the scale of production was much smaller and surviving examples are consequently rarer. However, because the quality is lower, the prices they command are not as high as their scarcity might indicate.

BRITISH MANUFACTURERS

In view of the fact that Britain led the world in engineering in the 19th and early 20th centuries, it is surprising that so few metal toys were produced. Among the few British makers was Stevens Model Dockyard, founded in 1843. Some of their toys were a mixture of wood and metal and were extremely well made. Many of those illustrated in their 1906 catalogue bear a striking resemblance to those produced by Bing, particularly the model submarines. The firm was extremely small and, unfortunately, it is rarely possible to find any examples of their work.

People and Animals

It is almost impossible to produce a realistic representation of the human or animal form in metal. Such toys, therefore, generally possess their own in-built humour.

The most interesting toy figures are those made by Fernand Martin. The humour inherent in many of them was often related to topical events. For instance, his Chinaman wielding a battle-axe was made at about the time of the Boxer Rebellion.

Lehmann also produced many toys in which the actions of the figures are of primary importance, whether they are wrestling with each other for control of a car, assaulting a taxi driver with an umbrella, or controlling a bucking mule.

The wide variety of animal toys ranged from beetles to sea lions. Their actions were generally simple, and movement was by means of concealed wheels. Lithographic decoration ensured a bright, eye-catching effect, achieved cheaply.

In general, these toys were made for a low-budget market, and while they find ready buyers today, they seldom command top prices.

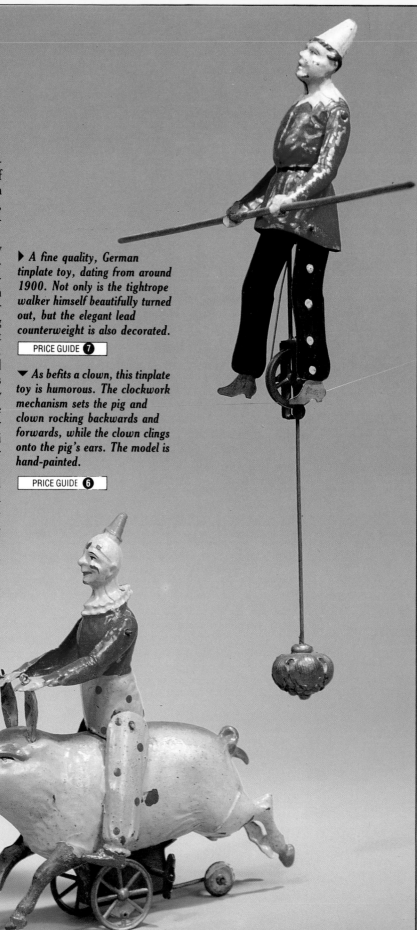

▶ *A fine quality, German tinplate toy, dating from around 1900. Not only is the tightrope walker himself beautifully turned out, but the elegant lead counterweight is also decorated.*

PRICE GUIDE ❼

▼ *As befits a clown, this tinplate toy is humorous. The clockwork mechanism sets the pig and clown rocking backwards and forwards, while the clown clings onto the pig's ears. The model is hand-painted.*

PRICE GUIDE ❻

PRICE GUIDE

Colourful circus acts and animals were popular subjects for mechanical tinplate toys. Tumbling clowns and acrobats, performing elephants, horses and dogs each provided amusing antics that could be successfully captured in clockwork models. Animals and figures were often finished off with fur and decorative pieces of fabric to give them a more life-like appearance than could be achieved with painted metal.

PRICE GUIDE ❹ ❻

Cars and Ships

Cars and ships were among the most spectacular commercial toys ever made. Some were extremely large, and had a wealth of detail lavished on them. Representing as they did the state of the art, many of the cars were based on very recognizable prototypes.

Even toys by the same maker varied considerably in quality, and it is those which were at the top of the original range that command the best prices today. Those most avidly sought-after are the ones with detailed modelling, excellent paintwork and added equipment in the form of lights and glass windows.

Ships were particularly detailed, with gun turrets, lifeboats on davits and gilded mouldings at the bow, for in the real world this was the period of great competition between the navies of the British and German Empires.

It was also the age of the great ocean liners and those, too, are often represented on a grand scale, although some were small enough for bath toys. Intended for use in water, sadly many have suffered the effects of corrosion.

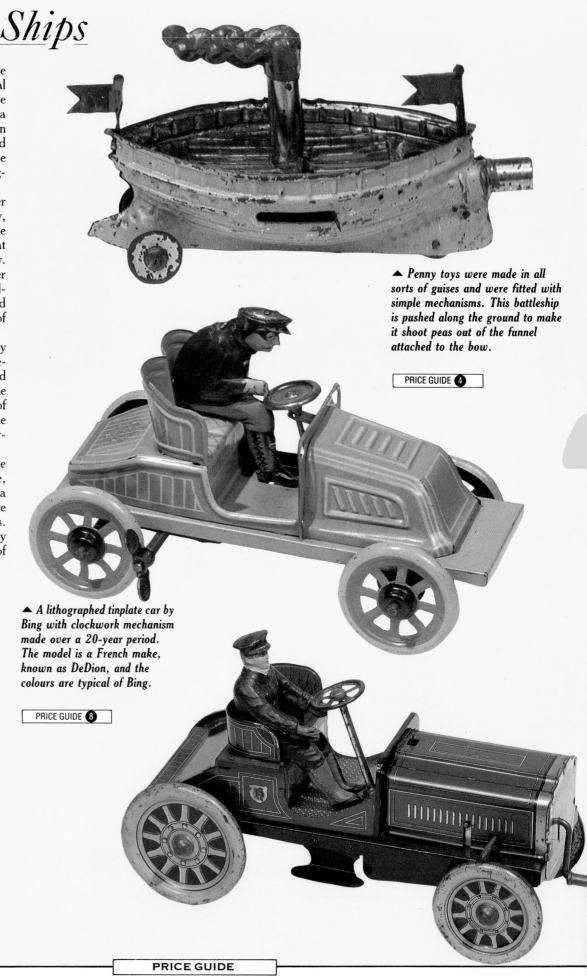

▲ *Penny toys were made in all sorts of guises and were fitted with simple mechanisms. This battleship is pushed along the ground to make it shoot peas out of the funnel attached to the bow.*

PRICE GUIDE ❹

▲ *A lithographed tinplate car by Bing with clockwork mechanism made over a 20-year period. The model is a French make, known as DeDion, and the colours are typical of Bing.*

PRICE GUIDE ❽

▶ *This friction-driven car with original plaster driver, by the German toymaker, Hess, was known as a 'Hessmobile'. The handle rotates a fly-wheel, which drives the front wheels. The brake is operated with the steering wheel.*

PRICE GUIDE ❼

PRICE GUIDE

▼ This rowing boat has a clockwork mechanism that motivates the oarsman and so the oars. Sadly, the oars have broken off and the paintwork is peeling with age. The boat is made by a company called Issmayer, which is better known for small-scale model trains.

PRICE GUIDE ❻

▶ The lithographed detail on this German tinplate car is in excellent condition. Made by Guntherman, it is a replica of an open-topped race car for the famous Paris to Peking rally (1907) – and is clearly marked on the bonnet.

PRICE GUIDE ❽

◀ With the changing design in real-life cars, so the toy models changed to keep apace. This tourer by Bing is a post-First World War edition. Open-topped and complete with chauffeur, car and paintwork are in pristine condition.

PRICE GUIDE ❼

PRICE GUIDE

COLLECTOR'S TIPS

Mark of Quality

BOTH THESE CLOCKWORK CARS HAVE BEEN LITHOGRAPHED, BUT THE ATTENTION TO DETAIL ON THE 'HESSMOBILE' STANDS OUT CLEARLY IN COMPARISON TO THE CHEAPER PENNY TOY.

The increased interest in toys over recent years has led to higher prices and a demand for items in good condition. When it was possible to buy interesting early tinplate for a few pounds, collectors were grateful to find any examples. However, now that good pieces sell for hundreds, and even thousands of pounds, it is essential to ensure that any purchase made is in the best possible condition.

VARYING PRICES

As with all collectables, the shorter the supply on the market, the greater the demand. Toys that were churned out in the Edwardian period and survive in considerable numbers today, such as Lehmann's Tom, the climbing monkey, fetch much more reasonable prices than the rarer items.

Cars are a specialist collectors' area in their own right and consequently the market is large and prices high. Hand-painted items may indicate an early model, as lithographic printing was only introduced in 1895, but this is not always the case. Hand-painting continued alongside lithography, but was usually carried out on the more special, expensive toys. Now, therefore, hand-painted items fetch higher prices.

One ingenious way that toymakers had of warding off competition was by producing toys over a long period. By doing this, the toymaker could very slightly alter a design detail, such as a wheel spoke, and so extend the patent. In this way, competitors were prevented from copying the design until the extended patent expired. These earlier examples of a model are therefore rarer and attract higher prices today.

It is seldom that toys survive complete with their original box, but if found this does add to the interest and cost of a toy, even if the box has been damaged. The highest accolade for a toy in the auction catalogue is 'mint and boxed'.

WHAT TO LOOK FOR

Mechanical toys are not often found in the ordinary antique shop. The best source of toys in reasonable condition is at the large auction houses, although these can realize quite high prices. For a wider range of toys, the major toy fairs are a good hunting ground.

When examining a prospective purchase, look carefully for signs of rust. Established rust is difficult to eradicate and, if left unchecked, can lead to serious deterioration, ultimately destroying the value of the

Lehmann's Auto-sisters

MADE IN BERLIN IN THE 1900S BY LEHMANN, THE AUTO-SISTERS IS A GOOD EXAMPLE OF AN AMUSING EDWARDIAN NOVELTY TOY. AS THE DRIVER STEERS THE MOTORIZED HANSON CAB ALONG AN ECCENTRIC PATH, THE SISTER IN RED ATTEMPTS TO BEAT THE DOG OFF THE STEP OF THE CAB WITH HER FURLED UMBRELLA. AT THE SAME TIME, THE DOG TWISTS OUT OF HER WAY AND THE OTHER SISTER WAVES HER ARM.

PACKED IN AN ATTRACTIVE BOX, LEHMANN MECHANICAL TOYS ALWAYS CARRY A PATENT MARK ON BOTH BOX AND TOY. ORIGINALLY THE WINDOWS CONTAINED CELLULOID.

① TRADEMARK ON THE ROOF IDENTIFIES THE MAKER.

② THE INDIVIDUAL SECTIONS OF THE TOY ARE JOINED BY TABS, NOT SOLDERED.

③ THE PAINT WAS APPLIED BY HAND, AS CAN BE SEEN FROM THE TEXTURE.

④ LADIES ARE DRESSED IN FABRIC SKIRTS.

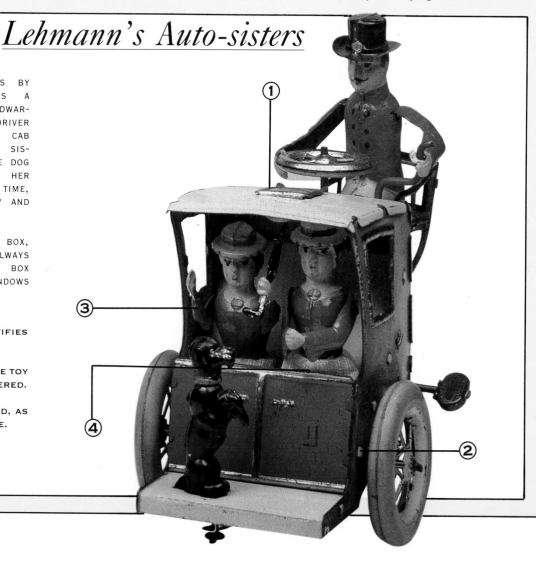

·CLOSE UP·

① **WEAR AND TEAR**

② **TOYMAKER'S NAME**

④ **USE OF FABRIC**

① WITH CONSTANT HANDLING THE PAINTWORK ON HAND-PAINTED MODELS INEVITABLY PEELS OFF. WEAK JOINS ARE ALSO LIKELY TO BREAK.

② THE TINPLATE TOYS OF ERNST PAUL LEHMANN WERE ALWAYS CLEARLY MARKED WITH THE COMPANY'S NAME. THIS ADDS AUTHENTICITY AND VALUE.

③ PATENT MARKS ARE ANOTHER INDICATION AS TO THE IDENTITY OF THE TOYMAKER. ONLY THE LARGE FIRMS MARKED THEIR WORK.

④ DRESSING UP TINPLATE FIGURES IN COLOURFUL CLOTHES WAS AN APPEALING TOUCH. IT MADE THE TOYS LESS MECHANICAL AND MORE TRUE TO LIFE.

⑤ LABOUR-SAVING LITHOGRAPHIC DECORATION ON TINPLATE TOYS WAS A POPULAR INNOVATION AT THE TURN OF THE CENTURY.

⑥ HAND-PAINTED TOYS WERE STILL PRODUCED AFTER THE INTRODUCTION OF LITHOGRAPHY, BUT WERE MORE EXPENSIVE, AS THEY ARE TODAY.

③ **PATENT MARK**

⑤ **LITHOGRAPHED DETAIL**

⑥ **HAND-PAINTED FINISH**

piece. The condition of the paintwork or lithography must be examined closely. While minor, almost invisible scratches may be acceptable, if it is seriously blemished or shows signs of bubbling, it is an indication that the piece has already been attacked by rust from below.

If the parts of the toy are joined by tabs, rather than soldered, check that these have not been opened at any time. This can be identified by flaking paint. If this damage is evident, it indicates that the piece may have been restored.

Test the mechanism gently. If a key does not turn, the motor has been overwound or has rusted solid. While this fault can be corrected, it is expensive and the cost of the piece should be proportionally less. Likewise, any moving parts or mechanisms should be in working order.

RESTORATION WORK

Such are the prices that can now be realized for toys that it is worthwhile buying interesting models for restoration. The work,

however, must be undertaken sympathetically, so that it closely matches the original paintwork and materials. When a toy has been completely overpainted or the wrong materials used, the work is less than useless and merely increases the damage. Well restored examples generally cost less than those in original condition.

POINTS TO WATCH

■ Look for signs of rust and check the condition of paintwork. Repainting can more than halve the value.

■ Ensure that the motor is in working order and movable parts have a free action, as these can be expensive to repair.

■ Check that tabs have not been opened or joins resoldered. These indicate restoration.

■ Where patent marks are visible, look for the last date. The toy will normally have been made within the following 10 years.

■ Always keep tinplate toys in a dry atmosphere; excessive humidity can cause corrosion.

▲ *A mechanical moneybank was a popular novelty toy. When a coin is placed in the hand of this Humpty Dumpty, he pops it in his mouth.*

Bisque Dolls

Of all the playthings available in the Edwardian period, the bisque-headed dolls were by far the most beautiful, and many have endured almost a century to become highly treasured collectors' items

The first years of the 20th century produced a greater variety of dolls than had ever been seen before. The principal country of manufacture was Germany whose workers were highly skilled after generations of experiment in the creation of beautiful, amusing or ingenious models to appeal to girls of all ages.

The fortunate girls brought up in a middle-class environment were offered a choice so vast that the contents of modern shops seem meagre by comparison. Cloistered in the schoolroom, they busied themselves with dolls for a much longer period than is common today. The sewing of dolls' clothes was considered a useful means of learning dressmaking and dress sense, so some exquisite outfits were made by teenage girls with the help of their mother or nurse.

HISTORY AND DEVELOPMENT

The commercial production of play dolls began in Ancient Greece. Some examples from this period have survived as they were buried with girls who died before marriage. Wooden, fabric, ivory and terracotta dolls were available to Roman children who adorned them with fashionable costumes and jewellery, though few examples of this kind are available to average collectors.

Since medieval times the country most associated with the production of ceramic dolls was Germany. Doll sellers operated mainly from market stalls and 17th century prints show that well-dressed models were available in several sizes. But for most doll collectors, the true history begins in the 18th century with the carved wooden dolls which were produced in most European countries.

Realistic models with shaped bodies were especially constructed for the display of women's costumes, and these were sent from France to the courts of Europe and to fashionable ladies in America to keep them informed of all the latest styles.

Play dolls were much simpler with skittle-type bodies and stick-like arms and legs. The heads were made from gesso – a type of plaster of Paris – and the faces painted with the heavily rouged cheeks and beauty spots fashionable at the time.

Moulded papier-mâché dolls were made both in Germany and France at the end of the 18th century, and with this material the heads could be modelled more realistically.

In the early 19th century, the new Empire fashions in thin, clinging fabrics necessitated the production of dolls with more realistic arms and legs, so the German carvers created jointed figures with coloured, flat-heeled slippers and flesh-tinted arms and shoulders.

By the 1850s, white porcelain heads, usually with black painted hair, were mass-produced in Thuringia in Germany. The bodies were made from fabric stuffed with sawdust, sewn by peasant outworkers, who also assembled and costumed the figures that were exported in great number to all parts of the world.

EARLY BISQUE-HEADED DOLLS

Early bisque-headed dolls were made from white bisque – which is a type of porcelain fired to the biscuit stage and left unglazed – and these are known to doll collectors as parian-type dolls.

Originally, these china dolls were made with leftover porcelain from the continental factories, and today many manufacturers are better known for their dolls than for their standard wares. Manufacturers experi-

COMPARISONS

Jumeau

THE FRENCH DOLL-MAKING FACTORY OF JUMEAU WAS FOUNDED IN 1842 AND CONTINUED UNTIL 1899. FRENCH-MADE DOLLS WERE ALWAYS MUCH MORE COSTLY THAN THE MASS-PRODUCED GERMAN PRODUCTS AND WERE SOLD WITH EXPENSIVE WIGS AND FASHIONABLE CLOTHES.

mented with colour and tinting, and delicate flesh tones were soon applied to the bisque. Shoulder heads modelled as ladies with moulded ringlets and curls became extremely popular, but these were soon discontinued in favour of more child-like representations which children preferred.

The shoulder heads of these new child-like dolls were provided with matching lower arms and legs, and fabric bodies stuffed with sawdust and attached to the bisque parts. They were then sent back to the merchants or manufacturers for costuming, usually in a simple cotton garment.

In the 1860s and 70s French makers introduced new methods of articulation and facial realism. The German makers were quick to copy them and were able, because of the cheapness of labour, to produce dolls

Edwardian bisque dolls make an enchanting and beautiful collection.

for a much wider public. By 1880, very realistic child-like bisque dolls were made with glass eyes, pierced ears and serene expressions. Bisque dolls of this type had chubby, infant-like lower arms, made of pink bisque, and bodies of white cotton or cleverly jointed pale pink or white leather. Moulded hair was discontinued in favour of 'real' hair, and long tresses of mohair made the dolls especially appealing.

The French were the first to use the composition body – a malleable material made from whitening, glue and resin which was moulded over wire frames and set to a hard finish. These bodies were immediately copied in Germany. The jointed bodies were articulated by wooden ball joints at elbow, thigh and knee, then the complete doll was strung with elastic. Bisque shoulder plates were no longer necessary and the neck section fitted a cup in the torso so that the head could turn.

By the 1890s all dolls were marked with their country of origin (few dolls were ever manufactured in Britain) and manufacturers such as Simon & Halbig and JD Kestner of Germany also incised their own marks on the back of the head or on the shoulder plates. French makers of importance were Leon Casimir Bru and his son, who made the original *bébé* dolls, and also Jumeau, and Roullet et Decamps. French dolls with bisque heads of this period should be stamped SFBJ for *Societé Française de Fabrication des Bébés et Jouets* with the mould number.

THE EDWARDIAN DOLL

Almost all the bisque-headed dolls made in the late Victorian period continued in production until the 1920s, though in more limited numbers. The most popular Edwardian examples were double-jointed versions with sleeping eyes and curled wigs, but shoulder heads on leather and leathercloth bodies were still made in some number for the cheaper end of the market. Various advances such as talking mechanisms were introduced for more expensive dolls.

There was great rivalry between the various factories and the doll-making families, and new ideas were pirated and prices undercut. The most prolific maker was Armand Marseille, a Russian émigré whose 'dolly-faced' products are now the most commonly found, but Gebruder Heubach, Simon & Halbig and Cuno & Otto Dressel also produced large numbers of similar jointed and leather-bodied dolls. The baby doll with bent limbs was very much an Edwardian innovation and pointed the way to the mass production of the future, as the bodies were press moulded and made of only five parts. Closed-mouth baby dolls, though originally cheaper, were made in smaller quantities than the open-mouthed versions and are now more expensive.

Idealized Dolls

Sweet-faced, idealized dolls, introduced in the 19th century, remained popular until the mid-1920s. All the German factories produced a wide range of models with open mouths, sleeping glass eyes and double-jointed wood and composition bodies. The same head, invariably smiling to show the moulded or applied teeth, was available in a large number of sizes. Armand Marseille factory-produced these dolls in quantity, and their most common model – with the mould number 390 – is found in all sizes from 7-40 inches (17-100 cm); the life-sized versions were often sold to drapers' shops as display models for children's clothes. Some of the better quality dolls have pierced ears for earrings and a few have slits on the brow so that realistic mohair could be pushed through. A few of the composition bodies are stamped with the makers' marks but these are more frequently found on the head, covered with the real or mohair wig. These wigs were the most expensive part of the doll and some idea of the original quality of the piece is indicated by the length and abundance of hair. Fixed eyes are more common in the early models made in the 1890s, as after 1900 most children wanted dolls with sleeping counterweight eyes. The colouring and modelling of the earlier heads is, in general, better, as brows were modelled rather than painted.

▼ *A Simon and Halbig doll with a composition body dressed in white voile with pink ribbon trim. The face is modelled with sleeping eyes and a partially closed mouth.*

PRICE GUIDE ❻

▲ *Idealized doll made by the firm of JD Kestner of Waltershausen. The bisque head is modelled with a partially closed mouth and sleeping eyes, and is impressed with the mould number 192.*

PRICE GUIDE ❼

▶ *Small blonde Kammer and Reinhardt doll with a composition body. The doll is dressed in white cotton with a broderie anglaise bonnet and satin slippers.*

PRICE GUIDE ❼

PRICE GUIDE

▼ *Simon and Halbig doll with a composition body. The partially open mouth has moulded teeth and the sleeping eyes have real lashes. The doll has a lilac costume with a matching hat.*

PRICE GUIDE ❼

◀ *Large Simon and Halbig doll with a composition body. The face is modelled with blue sleeping eyes and a partially closed mouth with teeth. The clothes are made in a popular Edwardian style.*

PRICE GUIDE ❻

▶ *Small Kestner doll with blue eyes and a closed mouth. The doll is dressed in a long pink frock with a matching hat pinned onto her straight blonde hair.*

PRICE GUIDE ❺

PRICE GUIDE

Character Dolls

Character dolls with life-like and natural faces were the most significant advance of the Edwardian period. The development began in Germany where doll artists, tired of creating sweet-faced models, started to experiment with frowning, scowling and pouting faces. The first bisque-headed character was produced by Kammer & Reinhardt and marketed as 'Baby' with the mould number of 100. The composition body, with bent limbs and with one arm towards the chest, was also more realistic. Buyers for the large shops were at first worried about such realism but, within a few months, orders flooded in and the new type, now in such demand, was imitated by other firms. Kammer and Reinhardt remained leaders and rapidly added jointed and toddler characters with names such as Marie and Gretchen. These versions are now among the most expensive and collectable of all German products. Some were said to have been modelled on actual children, in all moods from tears to laughter. Other firms made appealing characters in white, black and brown bisque and the coloured versions are much rarer. Several smaller factories introduced their own characters and these are now valued on their basic quality and the interest of the model.

◄ *Character doll by JD Kestner, mould No. 260. The bisque head is made with sleeping eyes and an open mouth with teeth.*

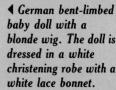

PRICE GUIDE **6**

◄ *German bent-limbed baby doll with a blonde wig. The doll is dressed in a white christening robe with a white lace bonnet.*

PRICE GUIDE **6**

▶ *Kammer and Reinhardt toddler, mould No. 122, c. 1912, with double jointed composition body and sleeping eyes.*

PRICE GUIDE **7**

▶ *George Borgfeldt character toddler, mould No. 327, c. 1920. The bisque head was moulded by Armand Marseille.*

PRICE GUIDE **6**

▶ *Gerbruder Heubach Negro baby doll, c. 1910, with a bent-limbed composition body and moulded hair.*

PRICE GUIDE **8**

PRICE GUIDE

COLLECTOR'S TIPS

Doll collecting is one of the most popular areas in the antiques scene, resulting in high prices and keen competition. Experienced collectors buy at the specialist auctions run by the leading salerooms, but the beginner is advised to purchase from a reputable dealer, as damage and faults are not always stated in catalogues, and the inexperienced could also be misled by reproductions. Doll fairs, at which most of the dealers exhibit, are held regularly in London, and both reproductions and antiques are shown. A few areas throughout the country have collector's clubs where knowledge, as well as price guides, are passed on to the new collectors. At first, however, more can be gained from visiting museums and reading specialist books.

CARE AND REPAIR

Bisque-headed dolls with composition bodies are among the least difficult to look after, as they are not affected by light and will not suffer in normal household conditions. Extreme cold can cause heads to crack, so if the house is to be left without heat in mid-winter the heads should be well wrapped for protection. Extreme heat can sometimes make composition bodies crack or warp, so that it is advisable to keep the doll out of the sun in high temperatures.

Minor body damage, such as broken fingers, can be repaired with plastic wood or resin compounds, but ask a knowledgeable collector or dealer for advice before starting work, as an expensive doll is often ruined by inexperienced restoration. Cracks in the bisque head can be professionally restored, though the majority of advanced collectors prefer to accept damage, as even the best restoration often fades and discolours after a few years.

ANTIQUE COSTUMES

With dolls in original costume, damage is more likely to occur to the clothes, which should be kept out of direct light to prevent the colours from fading. Ideally, collections should be stored in glass-fronted cabinets with sachets of moth and insect repellants. If the room is unavoidably light, muslin or museum-approved fabric can be hung on the windows to screen the damaging ultraviolet rays. When the room is not in use it is a

French or German?

THE FRENCH DOLLS MADE AT THE TURN OF THE CENTURY WERE GENERALLY OF A MUCH HIGHER QUALITY THAN THOSE PRODUCED AT THE SAME TIME IN GERMANY. THE FRENCH DOLLS WERE DRESSED IN FASHIONABLE COSTUME, SUCH AS THE CHARACTER SAILOR GIRL (LEFT) WHILE THEIR GERMAN COUNTERPARTS (RIGHT) WERE DRESSED IN PRETTY CLOTHES WHICH WERE MORE APPEALING TO YOUNG GIRLS.

The Baby Doll

THE MOST PROLIFIC MANUFACTURER OF CHARACTER DOLLS IN THE EDWARDIAN PERIOD WAS THE GERMAN COMPANY, GERBRUDER HEUBACH, WHO PRODUCED A WIDER RANGE OF CHARACTERS THAN ANY OTHER MANUFACTURER. THE POPULARITY OF THE BABY DOLLS MADE BY THIS COMPANY WAS PROBABLY DUE TO THE FACT THAT MANY OF THE INFANT FACES WERE HAPPY AND SMILING. THE MAJORITY OF DOLLS REPRESENTED EUROPEANS. WHEN OTHER RACES WERE DEPICTED, COLORATION VARIED FROM BEIGE TO DARK BROWN, AS IN THIS EXAMPLE.

THIS PARTICULARLY ATTRACTIVE BROWN-SKINNED BABY DOLL WAS PRODUCED BY GERBRUDER HEUBACH AROUND 1910.

THE DOLL HAS A BISQUE HEAD WITH MOULDED HAIR, INTAGLIO EYES (HIGHLIGHTED BY A WHITE DOT ON THE IRIS) AND A PARTIALLY OPEN, RED-PAINTED MOUTH. THE COMPOSITION BODY HAS REALISTICALLY BENT LIMBS. THE HANDS ARE SLIGHTLY CLOSED FOR A MORE NATURAL EFFECT.

THIS PARTICULAR DOLL, WHICH HAS THE MOULD NUMBER 7671, IS EXTREMELY RARE — FEW WERE PRODUCED AND EVEN FEWER HAVE SURVIVED.

① MOULDED CURLED HAIR PAINTED BLACK

② INTAGLIO EYES CUT TO GIVE REALISTIC DEPTH

③ EXPRESSIVE PAINTED ARCHED BLACK EYEBROWS

④ PARTIALLY OPEN MOUTH WITH PAINTED RED LIPS

⑤ SAILOR-STYLE RED FROCK TRIMMED WITH WHITE BRAID

⑥ REALISTICALLY BENT LIMBS

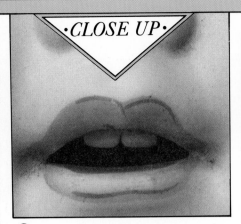

① OPEN MOUTH WITH TEETH

① MOST EDWARDIAN DOLLS WERE MADE WITH OPEN MOUTHS SHOWING TEETH.

② COMPOSITION ARMS WERE JOINTED WITH WOODEN BALLS AND ELASTIC.

③ AFTER 1900, MOST DOLLS HAD SLEEPING GLASS EYES WITH LASHES.

④ THE MOULD NUMBER IS FOUND ON THE BACK OF THE HEAD.

⑤ REALISTIC CHARACTER BABIES WERE MADE IN THEIR HUNDREDS.

⑥ THE COMPOSITION HANDS WERE ALSO BALL-JOINTED AND FIXED WITH ELASTIC TO THE ARMS.

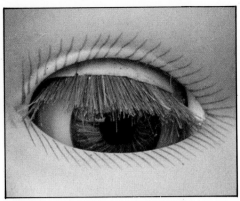

③ SLEEPING EYE WITH LASHES

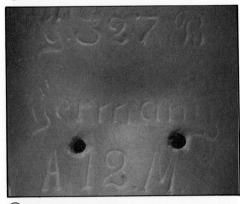

④ MOULD NUMBER

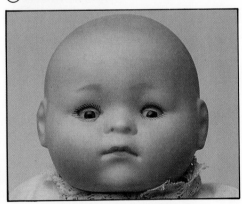

⑤ CHARACTER BABY

MODERN REPRODUCTION DOLLS (TOP) ARE OFTEN DIFFICULT TO DISTINGUISH FROM WELL-DRESSED ORIGINALS (ABOVE).

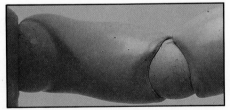

② WOODEN BALL JOINT

⑥ BALL-JOINTED HAND

good idea to draw the main curtains to minimise the damaging effects of light. Cotton clothes can be washed with care.

Antique silk and satin clothes should not be washed, as the colours may run and the fabrics disintegrate. Ask for advice from specialist restorers or the textile department of a large museum. Damaged costumes can sometimes be restored but the cost is often too high in relation to the total value of the object. If a new outfit is necessary, then use period fabrics and work from authentic patterns now available in reproduction and use contemporary buttons and trimmings. Keep the remains of the original costume in a plastic or cotton bag attached to the petticoat, as it might be of great interest to the next owner.

POINTS TO WATCH

■ Bisque heads are susceptible to damage, so replacement heads were common. This can drastically reduce the value.

■ Inspect a potential purchase carefully — even the finest hairline crack reduces the doll's value by half.

■ Sleeping eyes are sometimes replaced with glued-in fixed eyes — check that the eyes and mechanisms are right for the particular model.

■ Restoration can often be detected by a smoother area of bisque.

■ Many reproductions have been taken from original moulds and these are of excellent quality, although the bisque is generally smoother. Beware of unscrupulous dealers who sell reproductions as originals.

Many of the elaborate costumes were sewn by a child's mother or nanny.

The Scrapbook

The scrapbook was the delight of any Edwardian child, filled with every sort of scrap, it also provides today's collector with a valuable piece of social history

For the Edwardian girl, her scrapbook was a sort of diary. Many a happy hour was spent in the chintz-curtained, white-washed or prettily papered bedroom, picking and choosing from her collection of cuttings and assembling them in her book. For the young girl, this pastime was an outlet for artistic inclinations and satisfied her collector's instincts; keeping a scrapbook had a lot to offer as a solitary occupation for the middle-class child.

THE SCRAP ALBUMS

The scrap album made a perfect present for children, and even adults, in the days when people had time to spend carefully snipping, arranging and pasting. Handsomely bound, these books were made with printed or embossed pages facing the blank pages on which the scraps were pasted. Often different coloured pages were produced in dull green, blue

▲ *The more inventive Edwardian child might put together her own Christmas cards. Pieces of scrap and material were mounted on card with a message.*

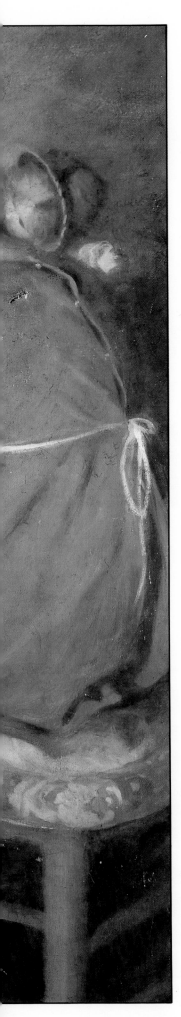

and reddish-pink. Tissue paper was used between the leaves to protect the scraps. These albums often had a colour-printed – hand-coloured in the earliest examples – title page, on which the giver could write an inscription.

Albums were imported from Germany, with the firm Richler, Tschuschner and Co one of the most important agents acting in London from 1882-1913. However, there were also many British companies making albums, such as George Chapman, established in 1883. The printers' names are often found on the title pages of the albums.

EARLY SCRAPBOOKS

The idea of keeping scrapbooks originated in the late 18th century, when ladies spent some of their leisure hours pasting verses and drawings onto the blank pages of bound books produced for the purpose. In the 19th century, making up albums was still an adult occupation, now indulged in by men as well as women, and by the middle of the century there was a thriving market for specially-produced printed scraps. These illustrations were all printed together on one sheet, but were designed to be cut out and arranged in albums as desired.

SCRAP SHEETS

At first, any colouring of the cut-out scraps was done by hand, but colourful printed scraps evolved with the development of printing techniques in the mid-19th century. With the invention of steel plates, very rich colour work could be done quickly and cheaply on printing presses, and the scrap business took off. By the end of the 19th century, there was a tide of printed scrap for all tastes. Making scrap albums was a hugely popular hobby, and was now largely confined to children.

The quality became higher with time. The colour printing was exquisite, with up to 14 different plates being used to achieve a range of shades. The sheets were embossed to give a three-dimensional effect, and glazed so that they had a glossy sheen.

SUBJECTS FOR SCRAP SHEETS

By the end of the 19th century, scrapbooks had become a typical child's hobby, so much material was designed for young tastes. Humorous sheets or comic cuts appealed to boys, as did soldiers, ships and policemen, while fruits, flowers, cats and ladies in fashionable dress were aimed at girls.

For educational value, there were illustrated alphabets, beautifully accurate illustrations of fish, shellfish and animals, and representations of current events and places of interest. Smaller children were attracted by nursery tales and birthday cakes. Children's names, illustrated with a child skating or cycling, were another popular subject.

EDWARDIAN SCRAP SHEETS

Printed scrap sheets gradually adapted to the 20th century. Often the embossing was less raised and the character of the designs changed. Children were presented in a less sentimentalized, less endearing

◀ *Friends and siblings spent many hours engrossed in organizing their scrap albums, often swopping spare or duplicate pieces of material.*

Sources of Scrap

▲ POSTCARDS FROM ENGLAND AND ABROAD USED AS SCRAP OFFER TODAY'S COLLECTOR A FASCINATING SOCIAL RECORD OF THE PERIOD.

▲ CHRISTMAS PROVIDED THE SCRAPBOOK MAKER WITH PLENTY OF MATERIAL, SUCH AS CARDS, FESTIVE MOTIFS AND GLITTERY DECORATIONS.

▲ LITTLE GIRLS WERE PARTICULARLY FOND OF MAKING UP MONTAGES AND COLLECTIONS FROM BRIGHTLY COLOURED FLORAL CUT-OUTS.

way, in keeping with the spirit of the time. Motor cars and aeroplanes were introduced as they became commonplace objects in real life.

The coronation of Edward VII gave scope for a series of new designs, but there was now a tendency for the paper to be of poorer quality, and inks bled, producing a fuzzy image. Quality declined noticeably after the First World War, when many of the previously flourishing companies of printed paper novelties began to close. Scrapbooks started to become throw-away objects of passing interest.

SCRAP-SHEET MANUFACTURERS

In England, most of the first sheets of specially produced scraps, either plain or hand-coloured, were produced by British companies. But the majority of the scraps that supplied demand at the turn of the century were produced in Germany. The printing works responsible were located in Leipzig, Dresden and Frankfurt. Importers, publishers and wholesale distributors flourished in the various European countries where there was a never-ending demand for paper novelties.

OTHER SOURCES OF SCRAP

Scrapbooks from the early years of the century provide a huge range of local colour as they were not simply confined to the printed scrap sheets. There was a wealth of other material suitable for a child's scissors and the swapping of spare scrap between friends was a popular custom.

Much scrapbook material was found around the home. This included such objects as Christmas, birthday and Valentine cards, which were carefully pasted onto the coloured pages of the album. Outside the home, omnibus, tram and train tickets were also candidates for the album. Some people collected

> ·PRICE GUIDE· SCRAPS AND SCRAPBOOKS

Completed scrapbooks can be purchased from shops specializing in ephemera, along with the individual scraps that made up the albums.

▲ *To accompany the postcards, magazine and advertising scraps, young girls often produced a painting for their treasured scrap albums.*

▼ *A scrapbook assembled with an assortment of postcards and advertising material, including billiard cartoons, Judson's glue, Parry & Rocke hosiery, is an interesting find.*

PRICE GUIDE 4

◀ *Postcards come in many guises, including plain printed ones, cards with decorations and embossed examples.*

PRICE GUIDE 1

them as mementoes of all the different routes they travelled – to school, church or on holiday.

By the Edwardian period, it was fashionable to send picture postcards to friends and family. Even an outing to a local beauty spot could prompt a postcard greeting to a neighbour, and these sometimes garishly hand-tinted cards were an irresistible addition to the child's album. Photographs, theatre programmes and even letters were also included in the book. Ladies' magazines, such as *Hearth and Home* and *The Lady,* were scoured for pretty pictures, as were department store catalogues, and children's publications, such as *Girl's Own Paper,* provided copious colour illustrations to cut out and treasure.

Advertising material also offered a colourful addition to a child's book, as embossed and glazed colour printing had long been used in a semi-promotional way. For example, little coloured cut-outs were stuck to biscuits and cakes for special occasions. These were also sold individually for the home baker to fix on her produce, and made obvious candidates for the scrapbook.

CUTTING AND PASTING

Essential pieces of scrapbook equipment were scissors and glue. A pair of cutting-out scissors were used, which were blunt-nosed and reserved only for paper cutting to avoid spoiling the edges of proper dressmaking scissors.

Paste was often simply made from flour and water, mixed up in old jam jars. However, the children from better-off families might have used commercial glue in glue pots.

◀ *A good way to keep old pieces of scrap is to assemble them in a modern scrap album.*

PRICE GUIDE ❶

▶ *Shapes and figures were often cut out from greetings cards to stick in scrapbooks. This is a chromo-lithographed Father Christmas.*

PRICE GUIDE ❶

◀ *Cut-outs from scrap sheets were joined together by tabs. Single cut-outs are fairly common, but whole scrap sheets are harder to find.*

PRICE GUIDE ❶

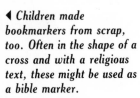

◀ *Children made bookmarkers from scrap, too. Often in the shape of a cross and with a religious text, these might be used as a bible marker.*

PRICE GUIDE ❶

Cut-out Characters

IN ADDITION TO THE POPULAR PRINTED SCRAP SHEETS AT THE END OF THE 19TH CENTURY, THERE WERE CUT-OUT CHARACTERS AND OBJECTS. THEATRICAL FIGURES OR FARMYARD ANIMALS WERE PRODUCED, WHICH COULD BE SLOTTED INTO WOODEN BLOCKS AND MOVED ABOUT IN TOY THEATRES OR PAPER FARMYARDS.

SOME PAPER CUT-OUTS HAD INSTRUCTIONS FOR MAKING THEM INTO THREE-DIMENSIONAL OBJECTS. VANS AND SAILORS WERE POPULAR AMONG BOYS, BUT A SMALL GIRL'S FAVOURITE WAS THE BABY DOLL CONSTRUCTION SHEET. EQUALLY POPULAR WITH YOUNG GIRLS WERE THE FLAT CARD DOLLS WITH PAPER CLOTHES, WHICH WERE FITTED ON BY MEANS OF TABS. SHEETS OF ADDITIONAL CUT-OUT CLOTHES WERE SOLD TO MATCH ANY SOCIAL OCCASION.

Money-Boxes

There is a special delight in finding an old money-box which has escaped
the fate of being reduced to pottery fragments or a tangle of tinplate

Edwardian schoolboys took the business of saving up pennies in a money-box very seriously. The virtue of thrift was instilled into them from an early age, but it was normally only middle-class children who received the regular pocket money necessary to practise it. Often this was no more than a penny a week, but from time to time their capital would be augmented by generous 'tips' from visiting uncles. The money-box where savings were stored was most likely to be a cheap, imported pottery piggy-bank or a bright red tinplate pillar-box. Few British children were as lucky as their American contemporaries, who were encouraged to save by splendid mechanical 'money-banks' with moving figures, which, like fairground amusements, gave some exciting action in return for a penny.

Since these exotic examples now change hands for large sums of money, most of today's enthusiasts of limited means will be forced to collect less exorbitantly priced money-boxes, perhaps pottery ones from the 19th century, or the great variety of tinplate examples produced in the first half of this century.

The idea of making a container for coins which put them effectively out of reach occurred to many ancient civilizations. The Romans, for example, made terracotta jars which were the direct ancestors of today's piggy-banks. The tapering neck of the jar was sealed at the top and crowned with a decorative knob, and the only hole in it was the slot for inserting money. If a mischievous youngster wanted to steal some *denarii,* he would have had a far harder task than the Edwardian schoolboy armed with a penknife.

Modern money-boxes in the shape of pigs or fish started to appear in Europe in the 17th century. Nobody knows for certain where and when the pig became associated with the saving of money, but the fact that pigs were traditionally fattened up to be

killed at Christmas or some other important festival made them an obvious symbol for investment towards future prosperity. For similar reasons, the hen sitting on a nest also became a popular shape for pottery money-boxes.

In the 18th century the Staffordshire potteries naturally included money-boxes in their vast range of wares. The most characteristic shape was the cottage, often with a man and a woman standing on either side of it. In many cases, the model was identical to one used to make pastille-burners, the only difference being that the money-boxes had a slot in the roof, whereas the pastille-burners had a hole in the back. Not all money-boxes were so decorative, however; there were still crude box- or egg-shaped containers with very rudimentary decoration.

VALUE AND DECORATION

The value of a cottage obviously depends on its decoration. Among the most sought-after are those in Pratt ware, with relief decoration, underglaze colouring and sponged bases, dating from the beginning of the 19th century. Money-boxes in the shape of castles and buildings intended to resemble

banks also date from about the same time. The latter were, however, more common in America, where the local bank played a much more important role in the lives of the general populace.

The Victorian era saw the production of money-boxes in many other materials besides pottery. Among the most attractive were decorated wooden boxes, some of them lockable, in Tunbridge ware or Scottish tartan ware. Well-made as they were, few have survived intact.

CAST-IRON MONEY-BOXES

More durable were the various cast-iron models, probably the first money-boxes to be made specifically for children. These commonly took the form of animal or human heads, their mouths open to receive a coin. There were also bank buildings and standing figures of people and animals with the coin slot in the top of their heads. Towards the end of the 19th century, many were cast in lighter alloys, and some were brightly painted, while others were given a bronzed or brassy finish.

Cast iron was also the material of the American mechanical banks manufactured from about 1870 to the early 1900s. The firms which seem to have had the largest output were Shephard Hardware Co. and J. & E. Stevens Co. of Cromwell, Connecticut. Favourite subjects included acrobats, bucking horses

◀ *A young boy gleefully extracts his savings from a money-box. As it has only one slot in the top, the pennies have to lifted out with the aid of a knife.*

▼ *This selection of 'still banks' in tin, cast iron and ceramic illustrates the wealth of choice available to the collector.*

books could be made of many different materials; often they were of printed tinplate held together by little metal tabs, so their life expectancy was short.

Tinplate was the most commonly used material for money-boxes between the wars, as it was for all toys until the advent of plastic. Germany continued to produce amusing mechanical money-banks in tinplate instead of cast iron, some incorporating a clockwork mechanism or even a musical box. A line that was especially popular in France was the vending machine, which rewarded young savers with a chocolate when they inserted their coins. Both types were exported in large numbers to Britain, where the money-boxes produced were fairly unimaginative in comparison – traditional pillar-boxes, cash-boxes and bank buildings being considered reliable favourites. The most interesting British products of this period, from the point of view of the collector, are the sweet and biscuit tins made by firms like Sharp's Toffees, Huntley & Palmer and Crawford's. Once the contents had been eaten, the child could use the tin house or telephone kiosk as a money box.

GOOD AND BAD CONDITION

One of the obvious problems confronting the collector is the fact that tinplate money-boxes are seldom found in good condition. Even so, they may be worth buying if they are of unusual design, and should not cost too much, unless they can be proved to date from World War I or before. Of ceramic money-boxes made this century, anything in Doulton stoneware is certain to be a good investment, and many potteries have issued commemorative money-boxes for events like royal weddings, which are sure to increase in value if looked after. Cast-iron examples from the beginning of this century are valuable whatever their condition, since they are very rarely found with all their paintwork intact, but what collectors dream of discovering in an old forgotten toy box is one of the mechanical banks produced in England by the firm of John Harper & Co.

On the other hand, collectors sometimes come across objects which are not really money-boxes at all; church offertory boxes, old collecting tins or the small bronzed safes issued by the Post Office Savings Bank in the early years of this century. These are never worth as much as children's toys, because their designs are dull and predictable.

and mules, Punch and Judy and a monkey on a barrel organ. Some mechanisms were operated simply by the weight of a coin, while others required the pulling of a lever or the release of a catch, as in the common type of bank where a soldier shot the coin from his gun into a hole in a tree.

One of the simplest of the mechanical banks was the so-called 'Jolly Nigger' or 'Sambo' type. This was the stereotyped head of a comic black fellow; a coin placed on his tongue caused him to swallow it and roll his eyeballs. Models of Sambo and his female equivalent 'Dinah' have been reproduced by many manufacturers in more recent times. There is no doubt that a good many of these have been artificially aged to increase their value, a deception which has been practised on many money-boxes.

The Sambo money-bank was copied at the time by British manufacturers, although usually as a 'still bank' with no mechanical action. Standing golliwogs were also popular as money-boxes.

Parents who were aware of the educational value of toys might have bought one of the 'register banks', usually in the shape of cash registers, which recorded the number of deposits a child made and rang a bell at the same time. There were equally realistic miniature safes with combination locks and money-boxes in the shape of books with a tiny padlock. The

▲ *Four American cast-iron mechanical banks. Pennies placed in the hands of Sambo, Dinah and Uncle Sam are lifted to the mouth and swallowed. The bear has his own dish for coins.*

The Edwardian Nanny's Room

As time went by, Nanny's large but cluttered bedroom would fill with the paraphernalia of child care and souvenirs of her years of service

The nanny – a senior and respected servant, as powerful in her own realm as the butler and the cook in theirs – was entitled to a spacious bedroom. The furnishings, however, had either seen much better days in the drawing room or in one of the family bedrooms, or else they were plain, cheap and decidedly functional. With an old washstand or a simple basin in the corner and a well-worn sofa, the room had something of that depressing atmosphere common to all bed-sitting rooms. This air of shabbiness was relieved by an attractive jumble of equipment related to the nanny's job and her motley collection of colourful ornaments, many of them gifts from her former and present charges.

It is not a room that many would want to re-create. The nanny of today – and her mistress – prefer a lighter, less cluttered look with more modern furniture, fitted wardrobes and white or pastel walls with modern prints, rather than the hand-me-down furniture of yesteryear.

Good, functional furniture of the period is offset by nanny's personal collection of framed pictures on warmly patterned walls.

◀ *When the children were safely in bed nanny might take a break from sewing to read a magazine.*

Few nannies married. In the household the only male servant of equal rank was the butler, and when butlers married they tended to think of their stomach and therefore married the cook. On those occasions when nanny left the house, the responsibilities of her job and a certain acquired snobbery tended to shield her from the attentions of men.

An essential item on nanny's excursions was the umbrella. On the handles of many Edwardian prams there was a long, thin basket which served as a quiver for nanny's umbrellas and parasols.

▼ *Nursery-maids wore a neatly pressed uniform. The starched collar must have chafed during the course of a long day.*

▼ *The pot-cupboard, which held nanny's chamber pot, stood beside her bed. This one is a late Victorian piece, made of oak, which would still serve as a handy bedside cupboard.*

The status and living quarters of the Edwardian nanny varied enormously from household to household. In a small, town-dwelling, middle-class family she might be required to stay for perhaps five years, and throughout that time she would sleep in the night nursery with the two or three infants in her care. Nannies engaged on these terms had to live more or less out of a trunk, before moving on to another position of similar insecurity.

In contrast, a nanny to the country gentry might well remain in the employment of a single family for the whole of her working life, having started out as a 13-year-old nursery-maid, terrified of the inviolable traditions and strict rules by which her predecessor ruled her domain.

Even when tiny feet were no longer to be heard in the house, and the day and night nurseries had been put to other use, nanny's bedroom would still be in the old nursery corridor.

A MANAGEMENT ROLE

In a large country house, the nurseries and the nanny's room would often form a separate apartment on the first floor not far from Mother's bedroom. Ideally, they would also be close to the back stairs leading to the kitchens. Child-rearing was a labour-intensive and messy business and a nursery-maid might easily find herself making 50 to 100 trips downstairs during the day. No such unpleasant duties fell to the nanny (or nurse, as she was still called in many families); hers was very much a managerial job.

If her employers were particularly rich and fertile, she might have an under nurse and three or four nursery-maids at her command. These underlings disposed of the contents of potties, cleared up accidents and sorted the dirty linen. Nanny could concentrate on pleasanter tasks, making sure the children were perfectly groomed before going down-

stairs to see their parents, or out to tea, or to church on Sunday, arbitrating in childish squabbles and, above all, overseeing nursery meals.

In the intervals between meals and other important duties, nanny could retreat to her own room, but there she would frequently be engaged on some useful task related to the running of the nursery: sewing, mending, checking the laundry or planning revenge on cook. Meanwhile, nursery-maids and children would often come knocking with some complaint or request.

HAND-ME-DOWN FURNITURE

Because of the frequent visits of the children, the fire would have a solid brass-mesh fire-guard and sometimes the windows would be barred like the ones in the nursery. The fire was not a grand affair, just a small grate with a tiled surround and a wooden mantelpiece on which stood a plain wooden-cased clock. There might be a trivet hob for heating a kettle

on the fire, or a little spirit-stove on the hearth. On either side of the fireplace would be fitted cupboards for nanny's clothes.

The nanny's standard uniform was a voluminous white dress and apron, so if she was always to appear spotlessly clean, she would need two or three changes. A nanny did not have to wear starched cuffs and a cap indoors as the nursery-maids did, nor was she obliged, as they were, to wear a straw boater out of doors, although she might well wear one by choice in the summer.

For her 'smalls', nanny would have a simple chest of drawers and in front of the window there would be a small, low dressing-table. The most complicated part of her toilette would be her hair, so there would be two or three glass jars, possibly with silver tops, for her various pins. She would own a good, strong, sensible hairbrush (this would not be of silver, but might be backed in silver-plate) and, of course, a clothes brush. Other toiletries would include a simple

▲ *Nannies were proud of their collection of hats, toques and bonnets. In summer, nannies might wear a fashionable boater.*

LIFE AND LEISURE
Children's Remedies

▼ The Edwardian era was still the age of the cure-all. Emerson's Bromo Seltzer, a Canadian product, was not only effective against headaches, neuralgia, nervousness and brain fatigue but was also a laxative. Formamint made similar sweeping claims, keeping at bay everything from scarlet fever to bad breath. Glass or stoneware jars are collectable.

By the turn of the century the germ theory of disease had become established scientific fact, so nanny and the nursery-maids waged constant war on any dangerous microbes that might be lurking in the nursery. Floors were scrubbed with carbolic soap and wounds disinfected with iodine. Many children's remedies, however, were decidedly antique, dating from the era of 'vinegar and brown paper'. Most minor complaints, headaches or biliousness, were put down to disfunctions of the bowels, so the nursery medicine chest was filled with an assortment of laxatives and mild emetics: magnesia, Epsom salts, senna leaves or pods.

The bottle for which nanny would instinctively reach at the slightest symptom of illness was that favourite medicine, castor oil. As Mrs Beeton's *Housewives' Treasury* put it: 'It is the safest of any to be found in the medicine chest, for if it does no particular good, not perhaps being applicable to the case in hand, it has seldom been known to cause harm.'

"Now, children, suck some of these tablets on your way to school, and coming home. Then you won't catch any infectious illness."

Don't let your children catch other children's diseases. No school is safe from sudden and dangerous epidemics. Protect your children—give them Formamint daily.

A physician writes in **The Lancet**: "School Medical Officers recommend the daily use of Formamint for children exposed to the ever-present dangers of school infection during outbreaks of Scarlet Fever, Measles, Influenza, Whooping Cough, Mumps, etc."

One of the House Masters at Harrow School, **Mr. A. Vassell**, writes: "Formamint has been very successful with the boys in my School House."

Wulfing's *Formamint*
THE GERM-KILLING THROAT TABLET

Besides preventing infectious diseases, Formamint Tablets cure Sore Throat, "Spongy" Gums, Tainted Breath, and other common complaints of the mouth and throat. These tablets are perfectly harmless, and so pleasantly flavoured that children take them eagerly.

Insist on Wulfing's Formamint—the *only* genuine kind—price 1s. 1½d. per bottle at all Chemists. For Sample and Booklet, please send a post-card—*mentioning this paper*—to A. Wulfing & Co., 12, Chenies Street, London, W.C.

We also make Sanatogen. May we send you Samples of both preparations?

▲ *The hairbrush and clothes brush were an important part of nanny's toilet set. These two Edwardian brushes have tortoiseshell backs and hog bristles.*

where she would have a little upholstered armchair, a faded fire stool and, if the house had electricity, a wooden standard lamp.

CARPETS AND CURTAINS

The decoration and fittings of the room also tended to be a little on the seedy side. The embossed wallpaper was not of the newest and the carpet was either a poor quality cotton imitation of an oriental rug or else a fairly threadbare hand-me-down from one of the family bedrooms. Similarly, the curtains would either be of cheap cotton or cut-down ones of better quality from another room.

Nanny's bedroom was never completely her own; the children would always come first. A prudent nanny would keep irons, curling tongs for the little girls' hair, the medicine chest and the first-aid box in her bedroom, out of the reach of the younger children. This would mean that children were never out of her room for very long.

NANNY'S CAREER

Children grow up, and the number of nannies who lived on with a comfortable sinecure into semi-retirement was very small. What often happened was

manicure set and a small pot of Pond's cold cream.

Among her few personal belongings would be perhaps half a dozen books, including a bible and a prayer book and some works on the subject of looking after children and their ailments. Mrs Beeton's *Housewives' Treasury* had a long section on how to bring up a healthy child. These books would stand on a little hanging bookshelf beside the bed.

The bed itself would be much better than those of the maids up in the attic; it might even have an old feather mattress rather than the sacks of lumpy flock endured by those servants addressed only by their Christian name. The wooden headboard and the board at the foot of the bed would probably be painted white and the bedclothes would have a quilt over them, perhaps with a patchwork cover she had made herself. Beside the bed stood that indispensable bedroom fitting, the pot-cupboard. This would be used even though the nursery corridor of a large house often had its own bathroom and lavatory.

Nanny's principal form of recreation was sewing (female servants were trained to be useful even when off duty) and to this end she would have her sewing machine. This would stand on a solid pine table which had turned legs, flaps on either side and a small drawer for sewing and darning equipment. The homeliest area of the room would be the fireside,

▲ *Kind-hearted nannies did not resent children visiting their room. Here nanny is reading a bedtime story to lull a sick child to sleep. If mumps or measles were rampant in the nursery and one of the older children also caught it, he or she might have a spare bed moved into nanny's room to confine the illness to one area.*

▶ *Nannies and nursery-maids were famous for their collections of sayings designed to instil a sense of morality into their charges. 'Little birds in their nest agree' was the principle that guided many a nursery. The children here, dragooned into their best clothes for a photograph, would doubtless have received many such strictures.*

that a close relative of her mistress, a younger sister perhaps, might be starting a family and nanny was transferred to look after them. By the time the cousins had all grown up and gone to school, one of the little girls whose grazed knees she had cleaned and dressed 20 years before might be married and require her services again.

This was obviously an ideal arrangement. It depended very much on nanny's loyalty to the family and on the curious fact that nannies rarely married. So much of their maternal feeling was devoted to another's children, that perhaps they felt no need to start a family of their own. In any case, opportunities for courtship were very limited.

The nanny who stayed with one family all her life would have done a fair amount of travelling. Against the wall of her room would stand her well-used, black-painted tin trunk, filled with clothes which no longer fitted, or dresses she had never dared to wear, souvenirs of some great love that never was, and packets of photographs and letters. Many of the letters would be from children she had looked after, written from boarding school or a holiday abroad.

On the mantelshelf old Christmas and birthday presents from the children and Gossware souvenirs of places they had all visited kept alive treasured memories. But nanny's greatest joy was when one of the young masters or mistresses returned to visit the family and she could admire the finished product of the education she had begun so long ago.

▲ *One of nanny's mugs. This one is hand-painted and made in Germany, as was much souvenir china.*

Nannies in Literature

THE FIGURE OF THE NANNY LOOMS LARGE IN THE MEMOIRS OF EDWARDIAN CHILDHOODS, WHERE SHE IS USUALLY REMEMBERED FONDLY.

LOOKED AT THROUGH A HAZE OF NOSTALGIA, THE NANNY HAS BEEN SUBJECT TO MUCH SENTIMENTAL IDEALIZATION, THE MOST EXTREME EXAMPLE BEING MARY POPPINS, WHO COPES MAGICALLY, WHERE PARENTS AND COUNTLESS OTHER NANNIES HAVE FAILED.

THE STRANGE BELIEF THAT THE NANNY WAS SOMEHOW THE 'NATURAL' PERSON TO LOOK AFTER UPPER- AND MIDDLE-CLASS CHILDREN WAS NOT HELD BY EVERYONE WHO GREW UP IN HER CARE. COMPTON MACKENZIE'S LARGELY AUTO-BIOGRAPHICAL NOVEL, *SINISTER STREET*, FEATURES A TYRANNICAL NANNY WHO HAS A MARKED WEAKNESS FOR THE GIN BOTTLE.

THE DANGERS OF LEAVING CHILDREN IN THE CARE OF A WOMAN FROM SUCH A DIFFERENT SOCIAL BACKGROUND HAVE FASCINATED MANY WRITERS. NEVERTHELESS, THE NANNY'S IMAGE HAS EMERGED LARGELY UNTARNISHED.

▲ AMONG FICTIONAL NANNIES, ONE OF THE MOST FAMOUS, NANA IN *PETER PAN*, CAME NOT FROM A DIFFERENT CLASS BUT FROM AN ENTIRELY DIFFERENT SPECIES. SHE WAS, OF COURSE, A DOG, BUT THE DARLING FAMILY SEEMED SATISFIED WITH HER SERVICES.

SHE IS SEEN HERE CARRYING MICHAEL, IN AN ILLUSTRATION BY ALICE B. WOODWARD. J. M. BARRIE'S PLAY WAS FIRST STAGED IN 1904.

▲ MARY POPPINS WAS A FICTIONAL NANNY WHO WAS OUT OF THE ORDINARY. NOT PARTICULARLY SWEET-NATURED, SHE NEVERTHELESS HAD A WAY OF MAKING MAGICAL THINGS HAPPEN THAT ENDEARED HER TO YOUNG JANE AND MICHAEL BATES WHOM SHE LOOKED AFTER.

◀ THIS PAINTING OF 'BEDTIME' BY DOROTHY FITCHEW EPITOMIZES THE WAY THE NANNY WAS IDEALIZED.

Carpet Bowls

On days when the rain lashed down relentlessly, Edwardian holidaymakers kept themselves amused with a wide variety of games and pastimes

No Edwardian family would think of going away for a long summer holiday without taking with them an adequate supply of games. The late 19th and early 20th century was the heyday for all sorts of games enjoyed by adults and children alike and during this age of increased leisure these were an invaluable way of passing days of inclement weather. As well as games played for the benefit of the children, there were also indoor versions of adult recreations such as carpet bowls and parlour croquet, in which the children might or might not be invited to take a turn. These could be played in a relatively small space (unlike indoor tennis), and allowed the compulsive adult games player to carry straight on with the match that had just been rained off outside.

The grown-up enthusiast for indoor games 'came out' with a vengeance during the late Victorian and Edwardian periods, when frank enjoyment of frivolous pursuits became acceptable. Men and women regularly played tennis and went bicycling together, and while weekenders had once exhausted themselves hunting, shooting and fishing, now they exhausted themselves playing games, outdoors and in. In some cases a pretence of playing for the sake of the children was kept up, but often it wore suspiciously thin.

THE GAME OF CARPET BOWLS

Carpet bowls certainly fell into this category. They were not enlarged marbles (by Edwardian times, definitely a children's game), but miniature versions of proper bowls, with one side flattened to create the bias that gives the bowl its distinctive curving motion.

Their appearance in Victorian Britain reflected the growing popularity of 'proper' bowls, which was championed by the famous cricketer Dr W. G. Grace – a popularity that culminated in the Edwardian period with the opening of an indoor club (for play with full-size bowls) at the Crystal Palace in London.

Carpet or parlour bowls were normally 2 or 4 inches (5 or 10cm) in diameter, made of stoneware by Copeland's and other firms, and came in sets of six along with a small white ball called the jack. The rules were similar to those of bowls. The jack was placed on the far side of the room, and each player

▼ With the increased leisure hours of the Edwardian age, every opportunity was taken to play games and enjoy a variety of pastimes. While mothers did their sewing, younger members of the family amused themselves with whatever was at hand.

Puzzle Bricks

A POPULAR CHILDREN'S PASTIME, BUILDING BRICKS OFTEN HAD THE ADDED ADVANTAGE OF DOUBLING AS A PUZZLE, WITH EACH FACE FORMING PART OF A DIFFERENT PICTURE, AS SHOWN HERE.

▲ *Early jigsaws were made for instructional purposes. This one, depicting Prince Albert, has a patriotic flavour.*

was given two bowls of the same colour. Playing alternately, the players rolled the bowls along the ground and the one whose bowl came to rest nearest the jack was declared the winner. According to *Cassell's Book of Sports and Pastimes* (1907), forceful tactics were only permitted when carpet bowls were played as a team game: 'When the players are more than three they may be divided into opposing sides, and it is then legitimate to play so as to knock an opponent's bowl away from, or a partner's bowl near to, the jack.'

In practice, carpet bowls was a game for adults. Children liked more immediate and visible results, and tended to prefer German balls, a version in which the jack was replaced by an octagonal 'ball' or die, each side of which carried a number from one to eight. A player who succeeded in hitting the die with his ball scored the number which fell uppermost after the impact.

The label 'German' was a British compliment to German ingenuity in toy-making. It was well-deserved in the case of German billiards, an ancestor of the pin-ball machine which is still on sale today as a plastic toy. The version popular at the turn of the century consisted of a wooden frame with a little support that gave the 'table' an incline so that the balls would roll downwards once their impetus was spent. As in the modern versions, a spring at the side fired them through a thicket of pins and hoops, points being scored if the ball lodged in one of the numbered holes or cups.

INDOOR CROQUET

Croquet was another outdoor game so popular that it was adapted for play inside the house. In fact, several different versions were manufactured for rainy-day use. Mallets, hoops and balls came in various sizes, and the makers tried to anticipate all conceivable difficulties presented by the indoor terrain. Parlour croquet was played on a cloth-lined mahogany board equipped with adjustable screws to ensure that the players could obtain a level 'green'. In a different version, carpet croquet, the hoops were supported by flat metal stands that did not interrupt the run of the ball. And sets of table croquet even included cushions to place round the edges of the surfaces so that the balls would not roll off!

Among certain social groups, skittles was a popular indoor game. It seems to have been widely played in rural areas, and a good many farmhouses had their own skittle alleys. The game resembled modern bowling except that the ball was usually thrown rather than bowled along the ground (in which case it was known as Dutch skittles). The children's version, suitable for play inside the house, was called ninepins, but this was not as exciting as cupolette, in which the ball was attached by a string to the top of an upright bar, so that it could be aimed and swung through the skittles and back again, with greater or lesser success in knocking them down. Quoits too was played either as a vigorous outdoor game or in a quite restrained table version.

People with enough spare room could also play tennis indoors, stringing a net across a large table and hitting a little celluloid ball with wooden bats. In the Edwardian period, it was still a rather sedate game, and though moves were afoot to organize it,

EARLY EXAMPLES OF SPONGEWARE, THESE BOWLS HAVE BEEN DABBED WITH DYE USING PATTERNED SPONGES, THEN OVERGLAZED.

CERAMIC CARPET BOWLS WERE FREQUENTLY DECORATED IN COLOURFUL PATTERNS. THESE CIRCULAR DESIGNS HAVE BEEN HAND PAINTED, THEN OVERGLAZED.

THE TRANSFER-PRINTED GEOMETRIC DESIGN ON THESE BOWLS HAS EVEN BEEN EXTENDED TO THE SMALLEST BOWL, USED AS A JACK. IN OUTDOOR BOWLS, THE JACK WAS INVARIABLY WHITE.

there was no universally agreed set of rules; people were not even quite sure whether they should call it ping-pong or table tennis.

A popular, cheaper and more light-hearted alternative to billiards was bagatelle, another game with points of resemblance to a modern pinball machine. It consisted of a portable table, usually between 5 and 9 feet (1.5 and 2.7m) long, with an india-rubber cushion around the edges and a group of nine hollows or cups let into the baize surface. Using a cue or mace (a cue with a wide head that made it easier for a beginner to strike the call cleanly), players tried to pot balls in the cups, which scored between one and nine points.

Jigsaw puzzles, cards and board games were perpetual favourites. Chess, draughts, backgammon and dominoes had long been played by adults and children alike, but Bingo – in those days known as Lotto – was regarded as a pastime exclusively for children. Halma, sometimes less elegantly called

·PRICE GUIDE· EDWARDIAN TABLE GAMES

Edwardian table games have provided a plentiful source for collectors, though prices will vary depending on condition. Containers, in particular, should be perfect since it is these that will catch the buyer's eye when reselling.

▶ *A late Victorian table croquet set, complete with hoops and wooden balls, brightly coloured posts and mallets. The handsome stand is made of finely turned mahogany.*

PRICE GUIDE 6

▶ *This wooden desk-top-sized game is a simplified version of parlour quoits, in which nine rings were thrown over correspondingly coloured pegs fixed to a board. It dates from about 1910.*

PRICE GUIDE 3

▲ *A pine bagatelle board. The original steel balls have been replaced by chrome ones.*

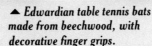
PRICE GUIDE 3

▲ *Edwardian table tennis bats made from beechwood, with decorative finger grips.*

PRICE GUIDE 3

▲ *A lithographed jigsaw backed with softwood. Its subject matter reflects the lighter Edwardian themes.*

PRICE GUIDE 3

◄ By the turn of the century, playing cards with court suits, as we know them today, were being produced commercially. Such cards are, unfortunately, of limited interest to the collector unless the pack is complete and in perfect condition.

Hoppity, arrived in about 1890, followed seven or eight years later by the ever-popular Ludo, whose Latin name concealed the fact that it was an Indian game; Americans knew it by its original title, Parchesi. Almost immediately after Ludo came another oriental game, Mah-Jong, which was all the more appealing because it was played with sets of picturesque tiles.

Some children's toys appealed so strongly to adults that they invaded the playroom and got down on their hands and knees with them. Surprisingly, one of these toys was the long-serving tin soldier. Right at the end of the Edwardian period H. G. Wells's *Little Wars*, published in 1913, enjoyed an unexpected popularity, and started a vogue for what we would now call wargaming. Having discovered the joys of massacring toy soldiers with a spring-powered breech-loader gun ('a priceless gift to boyhood'), Wells developed 'Little Wars' into a somewhat more sophisticated game with rules

governing the manoeuvres of Red and Blue armies through a makeshift country of paper buildings and twig forests. By modern wargaming standards, 'Little Wars' was a crude affair, but it met a need. As Wells himself remarked, it could be played 'by boys of every age from twelve to one hundred and fifty . . . and by girls of the better sort, and by a few and gifted women'.

Wells's breech-loader might have had a harder task if there had not been a technological break-through in soldier-making only a few years earlier. Until 1893, toy soldiers were solid, heavy lead figures, made in Germany and exported all over the world. Then William Britain pioneered a method of hollow-casting that made his figures cheaper as well as lighter than their German rivals – and satisfyingly vulnerable to Wellsian artillery. Britain's lead soldiers remained in triumphant possession of the battlefields, indoors and out, until the age of plastic transformed them from toys into collectables.

▼ This mah-jong set is made from amboyna (Indonesian wood) and has brass handles. Its sliding drawers contain bone and bamboo tiles.

PRICE GUIDE **5**

▶ This mahogany games compendium, made at the turn of the century, contains a threefold games board, a set of chess and draught pieces, 28 dominoes, a cribbage board, dice and dice cups.

PRICE GUIDE **7**

▲ An Edwardian dice shaker made from rosewood.

PRICE GUIDE **2**

▲ A solitaire board with 33 Nailsea glass marbles. This version was played with German rules.

PRICE GUIDE **5**

▲ A miniature roulette wheel and cover made of walnut wood and of Continental manufacture.

PRICE GUIDE **3**

◄ Ceramic carpet bowls made at the turn of the century. Unlike their counterparts made for the outdoors, which were always of plain wood, the indoor variety were often decorated in bright colours.

PRICE GUIDE **4**

The Spinning Top

After school, Victorian country children gathered together to play
games, often using simple toys which are still popular
with children today

Most of the games that children played in the playground, park, street or country garden were simple ones that had been popular with generations of children for hundreds, even thousands, of years.

Once school was over, country children gathered to play in the school yard or on the village green, common or river bank until it was time to return home for supper. As the days grew longer in spring, supper became a snatched meal and, fortified by hot tea and bread or toast spread with dripping, children hurried back to their games, to play free and unhampered until darkness fell.

THE GAMES RITUAL

Most country parents could not afford many toys but a great number of games needed only energy, imagination and someone to play with. Winter and summer, except in the severest weather, games such as tag, hopscotch, leap frog and king o' the castle were played, as they still are today. There were few hazards or disturbances, except for a horse-drawn cart trundling by, and a warning from parents not to play too near the river bank.

There were few toys available to country children and many were makeshift playthings made from whatever was to hand. A little girl's doll, her personal treasure, could, for example, be made by dressing up a clothes peg, while in the yard behind the village school, an impromptu seesaw could be rigged up from a plank and log of wood.

Some of the toys which children played with were purchased from a local fair or market or from pedlars who sold hoops and simple spinning tops. By necessity, children had to be generous with the few toys available and a number of games evolved around, for instance, the spinning top, in which a group of youngsters could participate.

THE SPINNING TOP

The simplest top was the twirler, a small wooden top spun by twisting the stem between the thumb and finger. An interesting variation of this was the teetotum which could be played with by a number of children. Made of wood or ivory, its sides were painted with letters or numbers and it was used like dice in games of chance. The teetotum was spun and when it fell, the number or letter uppermost decided the next stage of the game.

Although dice were considered wicked and Victorian parents were advised to keep them out of the hands of their children, inexplicably the teetotum was regarded as harmless.

Competitive games were also played with peg tops. To spin a peg top, the child wound string round the top and, holding on to the end of the string, threw the top to the ground. The string unwound, spinning the top as it flew through the air. With a bit of luck the peg top continued to spin when it hit the ground – so the child whose top went on spinning for the longest won the game. Peg tops were usually **made of wood (with hand-coloured patterns) and a**

Victorian Tops

SPINNING TOPS WERE MADE IN A VARIETY OF SHAPES, SIZES AND MATERIALS. THE SIMPLEST DESIGN HERE IS THE DARK BROWN PEG TOP IN THE FOREGROUND. THE SMALL, SPHERICAL HUMMING TOP IN THE CENTRE IS FINELY CRAFTED. IT IS FASHIONED FROM A NUMBER OF DIFFERENT WOODS, NEATLY TURNED AND POLISHED. THE LARGE, SUPPORTED TOP IS HAND PAINTED.

▼ *The art of spinning a top was something that had to be learnt. Here a Victorian country lad is proudly displaying the knack to a group of friends. A helping hand would probably have been needed to start the top spinning on his own hand.*

metal peg or point to withstand the impact of landing.

Peg-in-the-ring was another popular peg top game. Before many games began, however, certain preliminaries had to be gone through, among them picking the teams and deciding who was to start first. The peg top was then spun into a circle drawn on the ground. If it stopped spinning before it had moved out of the ring it became the target for the next side's top.

Whipping tops have been made and played with

Spinning Tops

THIS PARACHUTE TOP, MADE BY JACQUES, IS AN UPMARKET VERSION OF THE EVERYDAY TOY. MADE OF TURNED BEECH, IT HAS A BRASS SPINDLE AND COMES IN A PRESENTATION BOX.

AIR PASSING OVER THE HOLES IN ITS EXTERIOR CREATED THE DISTINCTIVE HUM OF THE HUMMING TOP. MANY OF THESE METAL TOPS WERE MADE IN GERMANY. SOME HAD A PUMP ACTION HANDLE.

since ancient times. In the Middle Ages, when such tops were rare in remote villages, a treasured communal whipping top was often kept for warming winter games which all country children could enjoy. To spin a whipping top, a leather, string or cord whip was first wound around a turned wooden top. The child then had to hold the top lightly upright on the ground and smartly pull away the whip. To keep the top spinning it was essential to periodically whip the top.

Supported tops, popular with Victorian children, were a variety of whipping top. String was wound around the stem to start the top, but to make sure that the top did not keel over before it had started spinning, it had a handle that fitted on top. Once the top was spinning the handle was removed. Supported tops were usually made of wood, sometimes painted or inlaid.

NOVELTY TOPS

More complicated novelty tops appeared in the second half of the 19th century. The kaleidoscopic colour top was a wooden top to which coloured paper or metal discs were attached. It reflected the Victorian concern for education and its aim was to show that certain colours mixed together formed other, different colours. Another novelty top had a pencil as the pivot so that, placed on a sheet of paper, the top drew as it spun.

Humming or choral tops, made of chromium-plated steel pierced with holes, 'hummed' as they spun, and this sort of top is still made in quantity for children today.

SIMPLE TOYS

Among the simple toys which children played with, the hoop was a top favourite. Children ran alongside it, driving it with a stick. Both sexes played with hoops and hoop races added more excitement, as did hoop fights where the aim was to knock down someone else's hoop without one's own falling down. Playing with a hoop was an energetic game that, like spinning tops, kept children warm in winter. The hoops were traditionally made of wood or iron, and were such simple toys that both rich and poor children had them. Sometimes in country districts the iron bands from beer barrels were used to make them. Hoops varied greatly in size, and in a family game, smaller children could jump through large hoops as they were spinning.

·PRICE GUIDE·⟫ PLAYGROUND TOYS

Few children's playground toys from the last century survive today and fewer still are in first-class condition. Sophisticated spinning tops therefore fetch high prices. Simple handmade toys, such as hoops and skipping ropes, have a rarity value to the collector.

▶ *Just as it does today, the toy shop window of Victorian times drew children like a magnet. The shopkeeper's display revealed an Aladdin's cave of new toys to hanker after. The children of prosperous parents could choose an elegant doll, a marionette, a model carriage or a conjuring set.*

The less well-off were more likely to settle for a hoop and stick (as the boy has) or one of the many spinning tops. Skipping ropes and balls were also within the reach of most children.

▼ *Metal humming tops were often imported. Those at extreme left and right are American made and cost 1/-9d. The others – also from the turn of the century – are German ones, costing about 6d each. The unusual black sphere is called a Lehmann's gnome.*

PRICE GUIDE ❹ ❻

▲ *Wooden handles on skipping ropes were not commonplace until the early 20th century. These handles have pairs of bells attached.*

PRICE GUIDE ❸

Unlike hoops and tops, marbles are still played by many children today. These were at the peak of their popularity in the 1860s and 70s, although children have played with marbles since the time of the ancient Egyptians. Marbles were made from clay, alabaster or steel, but some of the most attractive Victorian marbles were made of plain glass with swirls of coloured glass inside.

A popular 19th-century marble game was 'boss out', invariably played by boys as a competitive game and for which girls were considered too 'cissy'. The first player bowled a marble. The next had to either hit it or get so close that he could touch both marbles with one hand. If he failed his marble became the target for the next player.

Girls played a less aggressive game with five-stones. Also called knucklebones, these were originally small bones from the feet of sheep, but by the 19th century pebbles or pottery cubes were more common. The object was to throw them in the air, and catch as many as possible on the back of the hand.

Skittles or ninepins, still played in bowling alleys all over the world, were played by Victorian children of both sexes. This game began in the 14th century when it was known as 'kayles'. By the 16th century, nine had become the standard number of skittles and they were arranged in three rows of three. Victorian skittles were usually plain or decorated wooden pegs, although they were also sometimes in the form of turned and painted soldiers or even felt rabbits. One advantage of skittles was that, in severe weather, they could be played indoors or under shelter, as could popular ball games such as ball-and-stick and ball-and-cup.

Victorian ingenuity was also applied to skipping ropes. Before the 19th century skipping ropes did not have handles – they were simply knotted at the ends. Wooden handles were added to make the rope easier to hold. In Yorkshire the handles were often made from the wooden bobbins that were used in the wool mills. As still happens today, children recited rhymes as they skipped:

'Up and down the ladder wall
Ha'penny loaf to feed us all;
A bit for you, and a bit for me.
And a bit for Punch and Judy.'

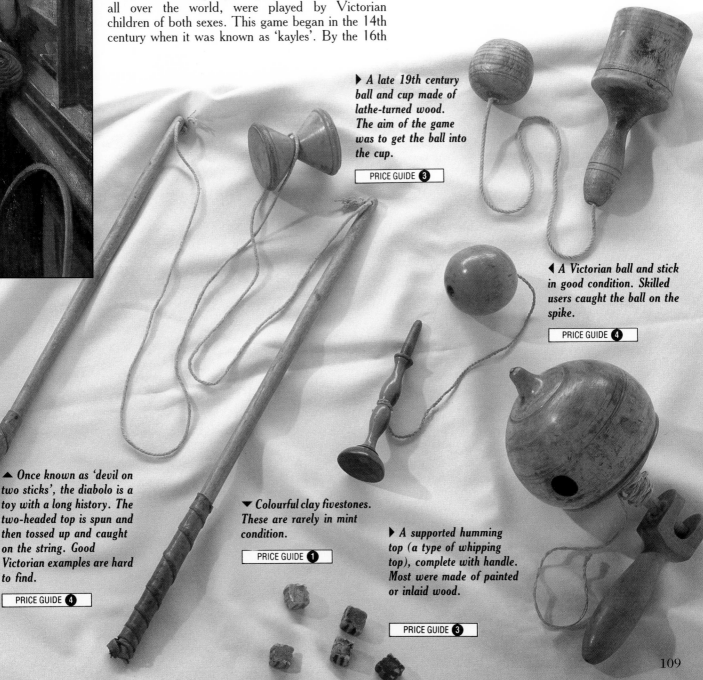

▶ A late 19th century ball and cup made of lathe-turned wood. The aim of the game was to get the ball into the cup.

PRICE GUIDE ❸

◀ A Victorian ball and stick in good condition. Skilled users caught the ball on the spike.

PRICE GUIDE ❹

▲ Once known as 'devil on two sticks', the diabolo is a toy with a long history. The two-headed top is spun and then tossed up and caught on the string. Good Victorian examples are hard to find.

PRICE GUIDE ❹

▼ Colourful clay fivestones. These are rarely in mint condition.

PRICE GUIDE ❶

▶ A supported humming top (a type of whipping top), complete with handle. Most were made of painted or inlaid wood.

PRICE GUIDE ❸

109

The Comic

Filled with well-loved characters, comics and annuals played a vital part in the leisure hours of the schoolboy, who avidly followed the exploits of his chosen hero from week to week

In the decade before World War II, before the advent of television, children's comics enjoyed a Golden Age, with hundreds of titles vying for the twopenny pocket money of children looking for laughter and thrills.

To some, a favourite comic was boon companion and friend, something to look forward to every week, to hoard and to treasure. To others, comics were the currency of the playground, assets to be bartered and converted into other comics, toys or sweets. To all children though, comics were principally something to be enjoyed, whether read as part of a Saturday morning ritual, devoured piecemeal in snatched glimpses beneath the lid of a school desk, or pored over beneath the bedcovers by the light of a torch.

THE FIRST COMICS

There were no children's comics in existence for most of the Victorian era. Indeed, very little of anything was specifically produced for children, though the 1870 Education Act had so much improved literacy that there was a great demand for reading matter. Children turned to penny dreadfuls, cheaply printed pamphlets with a close-packed text that had been produced since the 1830s to cater for lovers of blood and thunder. They featured notorious criminals such as Dick Turpin or Jack Shepherd, and spared no lurid details in their accounts of real or imagined mayhem. To counter these rather unwholesome influences the *Boys' Own Paper* was introduced by the Religious Tract Society in 1879.

The prototypes for the humorous comics known today were *Funny Folks,* a cartoon weekly with humorous text, printed from 1874 to 1894, and *Ally Sloper's Half-Holiday,* first published in 1884. Ally, a disreputable, drunken lowlife with a nice line in cynicism, had first appeared in Punch's sister paper, *Judy.* His new magazine had woodcut cartoons and strips, jokes and funny stories and was aimed squarely at the ever-increasing breed of office boys and junior clerks.

Then, in 1890, Alfred Harmsworth published the first issues of *Comic Cuts* and *Illustrated Chips,* similar to Ally Sloper but at half the price – a halfpenny. The pair soon built up a circulation of over half a million and were followed by *Wonder* in 1892 and a series of teenage boys' story papers – *The Marvel* in 1893, *Union Jack* and *Pluck* in 1894, *Boy's Friend* in 1895, all at the same low price. Their success prompted A. A. Milne's remark that Harmsworth had killed off the penny dreadfuls by producing the halfpenny dreadfuller.

In 1896 *Illustrated Chips* introduced the two tramps, Weary Willie and Tired Tim, on to their front cover in a weekly strip drawn by Tom Browne. This was the first long running humorous strip – it survived until *Chips* folded in 1953 – and Tom

▼ *One of the Big Five twopenny comics published by D. C. Thomson, the* Hotspur, *switched to a comic strip format before finally closing in the 1970s.*

Browne's clean, simple drawings, in contrast to the fussily detailed cartoons then popular, set a style that persists to this day.

COLOUR COMICS

Harmsworth also produced the first colour comic, *Puck,* in 1904. Colour comics always cost twice as much as their plain counterparts, known as 'blacks'. It was not until 1914 that the first comic aimed specifically at children, *Rainbow,* was published, featuring as its cover stars Tiger Tim and the Bruin Boys. After that, new children's comics appeared at the rate of two or three every year, each one launched with an appropriate fanfare and a free gift such as a balloon, toffees, sweets, a cardboard cutout toy, whoopee mask or a whistle.

STORY PAPERS

In the 1920s and 1930s, comics and story papers existed side by side. About half of the humorous comics were strips, with text captions running underneath the frames, and half were light-hearted text stories. The story papers ran illustrated stories and serials as well as non-fiction articles.

Children could be hooked on humorous comics from an early age, starting in the nursery with *Tiny Tots* and *Chicks Own,* then moving on through *Rainbow, Sunbeam* or *Playbox* to *Crackers, Happy Days, Jingles, Dazzler, Film Fun* and a host of others. Though girls' titles such as *Girls Own Paper* and *School Friend* were widely read, story papers were mainly for boys and catered for all classes of reader.

Boy's Own Paper, by now a monthly, with its colour plates and emphasis on Christian values, scouting, army life, practical advice and adventure

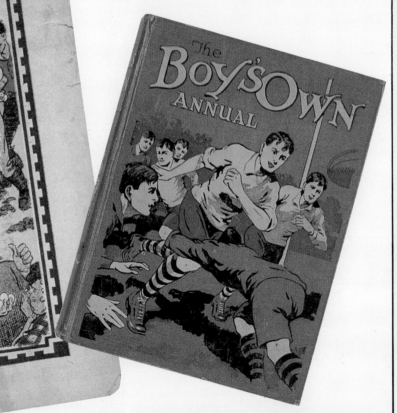

▲ *Original* Boy's Own *annuals collected a year's issues. Later editions contained new material.*

IN THE 1930s COMICS WERE USUALLY IN BLACK AND WHITE. TEXT CAPTIONS RAN BENEATH THE STRIPS AND THE MASTHEAD FEATURED THE STARS.

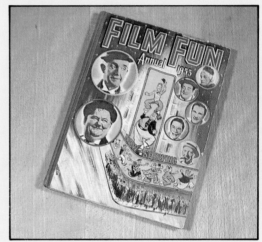

THIS ANNUAL FROM 1955 CARRIED NEW STORIES OF ALL THE OLD FAVOURITES, MANY OF WHOM WERE NOW STARS ONLY ON SATURDAY MORNING.

BY THE 1960s, *FILM FUN* HAD FOLLOWED THE TREND INTO TWO-COLOUR PRINTING, LOST THE TEXT CAPTIONS, AND FEATURED CARTOONS.

stories in the tradition of R. M. Ballantyne and Robert Louis Stevenson, was top of the tree.

Next came weeklies such as *Gem, Magnet* and *Boy's Friend,* mostly concentrating on stories of public school life. Every issue was almost entirely the work of Charles Hamilton, one of the most prolific writers of all time. He wrote about Tom Merry and St Jim's under his own name in *Gem* and about Greyfriars as Frank Richards in the *Magnet.*

Then there were the tuppenny bloods, led by the Big 5 of the Scottish firm D. C. Thomson – *Rover, Wizard, Hotspur, Adventure* and *Skipper.* They were a heady mixture of adventure, school stories, science fiction, westerns, sport and detective tales.

THE NEW BREED OF COMIC
At the end of the 1930s D. C. Thomson revolutionized the humorous comic with the launches of the *Dandy* in 1937, the *Beano* in 1938 and the short-lived *Magic* in 1939.

They dispensed with text captions under the strips and introduced a rough and ready knockabout style involving slapstick beatings, a revelling in gluttony and, in characters like Desperate Dan and Lord Snooty, an anarchic disdain for authority that struck an immediate chord with children and led Amalgamated Press – which Harmsworth's empire had become – to hit back with the similar *Radio Fun* and *Knockout.*

COMIC HEROES
Some characters took on a life of their own, and even switched from comic to comic. Billy Bunter, who began life as a minor character in the *Greyfriars* saga in 1908, was featured in *Magnet* until it closed in

▲ *With their larger-than-life images and action-packed stories, comics exerted a powerful hold on young imaginations.*

·PRICE GUIDE·❯❯ COMICS AND ANNUALS

◀ *Mickey Mouse* **Comic had a revolutionary effect when launched in the late 1930s. The first comic produced by the four colour photogravure process, its bright, glossy pages were an influence on post-war successes such as the *Eagle*. Both the comic and annual featured several Disney characters.**

PRICE GUIDE ❶

◀▲ *Puck, first published in 1904, was the first colour comic; Rainbow copied the format and its main character, Tiny Tim, took it into his own comic.*

PRICE GUIDE ❶

▲ *Teddy Tail was the Daily Mail's answer to the Daily Express's Rupert and the Mirror's Pip, Squeak and Wilfred as a weapon in its circulation wars.*

PRICE GUIDE ❶

1940, only to reappear in cartoon form as the cover star of *Knockout*.

Sexton Blake first appeared in *Marvel* in 1893, switched to *Union Jack* in 1894 and stayed there, acquiring his sidekick Tinker and faithful bloodhound Pedro, until it folded in 1933, when he took over *Detective Weekly*. Solving his cases not with Holmesian logic so much as a mixture of luck and pluck, he has proved the most durable of fictional detectives.

A contemporary of Blake's, Nelson Lee, began in the *Marvel* in 1894 with his sidekick Nipper, then turned schoolmaster, combining his detective work with school stories, and moved to *Gem* in 1934.

The World War I aviator, Biggles, began life in *Popular Flying*, the first of the aviation pulps, edited by Biggles' creator W. E. Johns. It was published to cater for the craze for planes among boys of all sizes. Biggles stories then appeared regularly in *The Modern Boy* from 1933 to the outbreak of World War II, when paper shortages spelt the death knell for many popular comics.

ANNUALS

Annuals actually pre-date comics; a children's book, the *Xmas Box*, published in the late 1820s, was probably the first. But the earliest comics had annual editions – *Ally Sloper's Christmas Holidays* was the first. Comics produced several bumper numbers a year: Xmas issues dripped snow and icicles from their mastheads, Easter specials were inundated with hatching chicks; holidays and Whitsuntide also produced double-length specials (at double the normal price).

The desire for more durable material led to the

A Bear for All Seasons

IN THE USA, COMIC STRIP CHARACTERS WERE DEVELOPED IN NEWSPAPER CIRCULATION WARS. THE TACTIC WAS ALSO TRIED HERE. PIP, SQUEAK AND WILFRED, THE MIRROR'S ENTRIES IN THE LISTS, ARE FOND MEMORIES, BUT THE DAILY EXPRESS'S RUPERT BEAR IS A FAVOURITE TO THIS DAY.

BEGUN IN 1920 AND DRAWN FROM 1935 BY ALBERT BESTALL, THE BOY-BEAR'S ADVENTURES IN NUTWOOD WERE COLLECTED IN ANNUALS, MONSTER ANNUALS AND ADVENTURE BOOKS FROM 1931 AND PUBLISHED WORLDWIDE. BOARD GAMES, JIGSAWS AND BADGES WERE ALSO SUCCESSFULLY ISSUED.

production of the Christmas or holiday annual, at first bound collections of weekly issues, later featuring all-new material. By the 1930s the child who did not receive the annual version of his or her favourite comic in their Christmas stocking could count themselves underprivileged.

▼ *Twopence could buy plenty of excitement in the 1930s. The* Wizard *and* Adventure *thrived on the improbably, three-minute milers and fiendish machines;* Gem *concerned St Jim's school.*

PRICE GUIDE ❶

▶ *Three annuals from the inter-war years.* Young England *copied* Boy's Own Paper, *all public schools and sport.* Chums *was wholesome adventure stories, while the* Rover *was more outlandish, a true tuppenny blood.*

PRICE GUIDE ❷

The 1930s Schoolboy's Bedroom

Sturdy, run-of-the-mill furnishings were the lot of most 1930s
schoolboys but few were without their share of the very latest toys
and games

An eight-year-old's room in the 1930s was, in many respects, little different from a young boy's room in preceding or subsequent decades. It was his private den, where he played, kept his toys and dreamt of being a hero – in this case, a cricketer, a footballer or train driver. It was rather the toys scattered around the floor that reflected the decade – up-to-date models of motor cars, racing cars, aeroplanes and trains lay amongst contemporary games and books and home-made

wooden ships. Light and well ventilated with large windows and plain but colourful walls, the room was very functional in its furnishings. A cast-off table and chair was the most likely, although those who were lucky enough would have had their very own child-sized pieces, either in natural wood or painted in a bright colour. When the room was tidy it might even look spacious but with father's cigarette cards and pictures of favourite sporting heroes, the room was typical of a boy's room of any era – havoc.

*With its clean
lines, space
and functional
furniture, the
1930s boy's
room became
a role model
for three
decades or
more.*

By the 1930s, the days of children being seen and not heard were on the way out. Although it would be some time yet before they enjoyed the freedom of modern times, children of the inter-war period were definitely beginning to play a more prominent role in family life. Domestic service had declined since the First World War and the number of families with a nanny to look after the youngsters was decreasing, having reached a peak in the latter part of the 19th century. Even many relatively wealthy parents had to look after their children themselves, and to do so became fashionable. There was too a growing middle class, forming a new suburban population. The trend away from very long hours of factory work towards more convenient office hours meant that people actually began to have the time to enjoy family life.

FATHER AND SON

Even father was encouraged to take more interest in his offspring. He did not change nappies, cook meals or do other household chores – mother still had to do all that unless there was a maid on hand to help – but he took an active interest in his children's education and in their development as young people. Little boys were encouraged to be like their fathers – a father was a lad's 'big, splendid pal', who taught him, played with him and even made toys for him, such as boats and toy aeroplanes.

Toys were not the only things father turned his hand to. A table which was not required elsewhere in the house could have its legs sawn short, making it perfect for the boy to use. Indeed, the furniture in most 1930s children's rooms was not purpose made. Better-off parents could, however, buy special children's chairs with matching tables in either wicker, which was cheap, popular and practical, or simply plain wood. A table and chair in tubular steel was a really up-to-date alternative – chairs with canvas slung back and seat were available for nursery school or home use and were light enough for children to pick up and move themselves. Children's furniture such as chests of drawers, beds and toy cupboards were usually made with rounded corners. Influenced by contemporary fashions for smooth lines, the lack of sharp edges meant that rough and tumble rarely resulted in injury.

SHORTS AND BRACES

The chest of drawers, again often in natural wood, housed the little boy's clothes. During the 1930s, shorts, held up by braces, soft-collared shirts and sandals in summer were the standard style of dress. Most women's magazines included knitting patterns for matching cardigans, one for fathers, and one, exactly the same but smaller, for sons. Little boys were encouraged to be little men, and mothers dressed them in manly clothes from the age of five onwards. A smart jacket was an inevitable item, though the pockets were invariably bulging with crumpled tram tickets, old boiled sweets, marbles

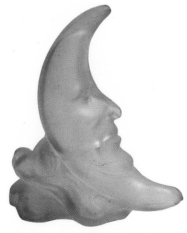

▲ *Much-loved nursery and fictional characters were always at hand, as in this night light representing the Man in the Moon.*

▼ *The 1930s schoolboy's room was his own private retreat. Here, surrounded by favourite toys and games, he could escape from rather tiresome schoolwork and parents.*

▲ *With the growth of industry after the First World War, there was a wide range of toys on the market. These children, outside a London store, are clearly captivated by what they see.*

▶ *Toy railway sets, which could be gradually added to, offered hours of entertainment.*

▼ *Children's annuals made useful alternatives for rainy days, but whenever possible the outdoor life was encouraged.*

and very many other 'valuable' schoolboy treasures.

Plain, painted walls were the usual form of decoration for a young boy's bedroom, with practical pastel colours such as green or cream as perennial favourites. Abstract patterns of cartoon characters brightened the bare expanses, stencilled or stuck on to the walls as transfers. Felix the Cat was one such character – a mischievous cartoon star of comic book strips who also appeared on nursery china. Also on the wall, space would be found for a map of the world, a considerable amount of which was coloured in red to indicate the extent of the British Empire.

In this somewhat stark room, curtains and bed covers gave a welcome feeling of warmth. Soft candlewick was the most usual type of bedspread with curtains often bearing typical Deco stripes or more cartoon characters appliquéd on to a backing fabric. In winter, the room was heated by an electric or gas fire. A few children might still have an open fire which was lit each evening and made safe with a metal fireguard placed in front.

SATURDAY MATCHES

Every other Saturday afternoon in winter, when the local team was playing at home, many a father would take his son with him to watch a football match. Those living in north London might well have supported Arsenal – a good choice, because Arsenal dominated the League throughout the 1930s, winning five times in all. They were 'a side that was horribly mean in defence and cruel in counter attack'. Father and son would head for the grounds and the boy would stand on his own stool at the front of the huge crowd, swinging his rattle and cheering with delight.

Back at home pictures of Arsenal heroes (or another team) cut from comics would be among the jumble of toys strewn about the floor. A Meccano set out of which almost anything could be built with its variety of metal plates, nuts and bolts, was rarely left in its box. Another company, Britain's, produced a most exciting toy – a model of the fastest car on earth, Malcolm Campbell's Bluebird, which topped 300 mph at Bonneville Salt Flats in 1935. Larger toy cars came in pressed and painted mild steel, and were often clockwork powered. Some of the best clockwork cars came from Germany, and were pretty sophisticated, some even having little mechanisms to stop them short should they reach the edge of a table.

A favourite toy – bought and also played with by

▶ *With their imaginative building ideas, Meccano sets enjoyed great popularity amongst boys. This magazine manual was an absolute must for all young devotees.*

The Boy Scout Movement

THE BOY SCOUT MOVEMENT, FOUNDED BY LIEUTENANT-GENERAL ROBERT BADEN-POWELL IN 1908, HAD, BY THE 1930S, BECOME VERY POPULAR.

THE BASIC PURPOSE OF THE MOVEMENT WAS TO TRAIN BOYS IN THE ESSENTIALS OF GOOD CITIZENSHIP, WHICH IN TURN INVOLVED THE DEVELOPMENT OF INTIATIVE AND SELF-DEPENDENCE, AND THE ENCOURAGEMENT OF A SPIRIT OF SELFLESSNESS AND HELPFULNESS. ORIGINALLY FOUNDED IN BRITAIN, WITHIN A VERY SHORT TIME THE BOY SCOUTS ALONG WITH THE GIRL GUIDES (FOUNDED IN 1910), HAD BECOME AN INTERNATIONAL MOVEMENT.

▶ SIR ROBERT BADEN-POWELL AT AN INTERNATIONAL GATHERING OF BOY SCOUTS IN THE 1930S.

▼ OUTDOOR ACTIVITIES SUCH AS CAMPING WERE WIDELY ENCOURAGED BY THE BOY SCOUT MOVEMENT.

father – was the Hornby train set, again made by Meccano, which he would add to gradually, building up his system of rails, clockwork trains, platforms, engine sheds, signal boxes and signals. If there wasn't a room to keep it in, it would all be kept under the bed, to be pulled out on most rainy days.

There were toy soldiers in lead, painted in regimental colours. In keeping with the vain hopes of the time that the world had done with war, there were alternatives to soldiers; farmyards with their lead animals, shops and circuses.

Games included Belisha, a card game intended to help with road safety awareness; it was produced 'with a sincere desire to make a helpful contribution to the Safety First campaign'. Cars were getting faster, and more numerous. The roads were becoming dangerous. The Safety First Association awarded prizes of half-a-crown to five guineas for youngsters' essays on topics like 'How would you take care of your little brother or sister crossing the road?'

In the 1930s, two great comics, the *Dandy* and the *Beano,* put in their first appearances. A comic that had been around a little longer – since early in the century – was the *Magnet.* In the *Magnet* could be found The Fat Owl of Greyfriars – Billy Bunter. Described by Frank Richards, Bunter's adventures at Greyfriars with his chums Harry Wharton and others and the beastly – but fair – form-master Mr Quelch amused and excited a generation of youngsters in the 1930s, as well as their parents before them and their children after.

Other books likely to be found in the lad's room featured the adventures of Rupert Bear, Just William and Winnie-the-Pooh. But he was encouraged to enjoy the healthy air outside as well as to read his books, and signs of this would be around the room – dirty football boots, nature books and model boats which he would take with him to sail on the boating lake when he and father went to the park with the dog.

But all was not idyllic – the 1930s was an unsettled decade, what with the emergence of the Nazis and the Youth Movement in Germany. Everyone knew that conflict was always a possibility, and family life was disrupted everywhere in September 1939 when war broke out. The boy's somewhat idyllic and cosy home life was soon ended as his parents worked for the war effort and he was shipped away – evacuated to a wartime home in the country for extra safety.

Toys and Games

Names of toys familiar to generations of schoolboys – Meccano,
Monopoly, Dinky and Hornby among them – were at the forefront of a
vibrant era of toymaking between the wars

The toys of the inter-war years reflected the mood and innovations of the time. Boys were fascinated by the exciting discoveries made in aviation and other transport, and toymakers were quick to respond to their interests. Using ever more sophisticated methods of production, manufacturers created a dazzling selection of toys at prices that could be afforded by most levels of society.

English toy manufacturers had, however, been slow to match their continental competitors. At the turn of the century, the toy industry had been dominated by Germany. Firms like Bing, Lehmann and Märklin were the best-known manufacturers of tinplate mechanical toys, and English companies like Bassett-Lowke were obliged to work in harness with them. It was only during the Great War that this dependence on German imports was broken.

By the 1930s, the mechanized figures popularized by the Germans had passed their heyday. In their place, there was a huge increase in demand for model kits, spearheaded by the new designs of firms like Bassett-Lowke and Meccano. Meccano itself was first patented in 1901.

KIT TOYS

Assembly toys had existed in England, in a fairly crude form, since about 1870. However, Frank Hornby's invention of the Meccano system – perforated metal parts held together by nuts and bolts – constituted the first genuine constructional kit.

Initially, kits were not used purely as toys. During World War I, many of Bassett-Lowke's products were used for training purposes by the armed forces. And, in the 1920s and 1930s, Citroën marketed miniature car assembly kits as promotional material for the real cars.

Soon, however, the craze was in full swing, with aviation the most popular subject. Lindbergh's solo transatlantic flight in 1927 sparked off numerous 'Spirit of St Louis' kits and, in the 1930s, as Europe prepared for war, military aircraft became very popular. Metal was, naturally, the sturdiest medium for these kits, although wooden and cardboard variants were also widely available.

THE ARRIVAL OF DINKY

After World War I, Meccano and Bassett-Lowke swiftly expanded into train sets, hitherto a predominantly German industry, and, from there, they diversified into other forms of transport.

Meccano's great invention of the 1930s – Dinky models – happened largely by accident. In 1932, a small series of 'modelled miniature' vehicles was introduced, purely as accessories for the company's train sets. Almost immediately, Meccano realized they had a winner on their hands and, by 1934, the Dinky line was born.

The range of Dinky models multiplied at an astonishing rate. Ships of the British navy appeared in 1934 and aircraft and military vehicles in camouflage colours followed later in the decade. Dinky also made a less memorable attempt to break into the girls' toy market with 'Dolly Varden's' range of doll's houses and furniture, using the same kind of die-cast miniatures.

Meccano's marketing procedure was

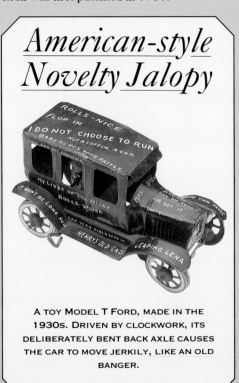

American-style Novelty Jalopy

A TOY MODEL T FORD, MADE IN THE 1930S. DRIVEN BY CLOCKWORK, ITS DELIBERATELY BENT BACK AXLE CAUSES THE CAR TO MOVE JERKILY, LIKE AN OLD BANGER.

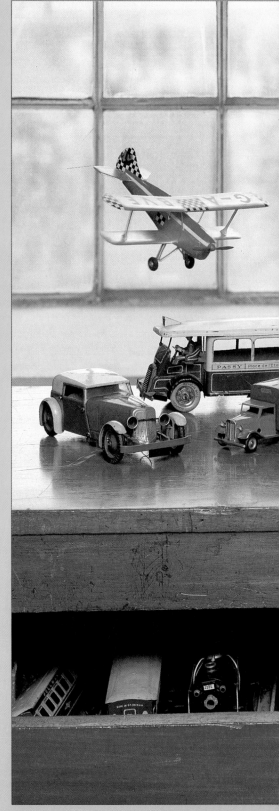

▶ *The toyshop of the 1930s was full of model cars, planes and trains which – as always – appealed as much to fathers as sons.*

based on selling their models both as sets and individually. An early set of eight cars, for example, cost 6/6d, while single cars could be bought for 9d or 1/- each. In this way, children could make the smaller purchases themselves, while hoping to receive the boxed sets as presents from parents or relatives. Needless to say, these boxed sets are now prized by collectors.

Sales were also stimulated by *Meccano Magazine*, which began in 1916 as a free, 4-page leaflet and continued throughout the firm's history. During the 1930s, an 'Air News' section on new developments in aviation technology was regularly featured alongside pictures of the latest model aircraft.

TOY SOLDIERS

Britain's were the principal manufacturers of toy soldiers in this country and, like Dinky, they made efforts to sell their toys in boxed sets, in order to encourage boys to build up large, thematic collections. During the 1930s, cavalry were available in boxes of five and infantry in boxes of eight or ten.

Britain's also produced extensive, well-illustrated catalogues and this gave them a distinct advantage over their smaller rivals, who frequently relied on skimpy brochures that could only be obtained by retailers. Many of these catalogues have been reprinted in recent years and are an invaluable guide for collectors.

By a cruel irony, the model soldier industry was severely hit during both World Wars, when the manufacturers' resources were diverted into making munitions for the real conflict. Many of the smaller firms foundered in the Depression of the Twenties. By the 1930s, only Johillco, a London company, challenged the supremacy of Britain's.

Metal toys were not, of course, the only thing that appealed to boys in the 1930s. There were the evergreen favourites, such as card games and puzzles, and new board games appeared, including Monopoly. However, the planes and cars produced during those years have a timeless charm and, more than any other toys, succeed in evoking the flavour of the period.

▼ *New toys are always being brought out to suit the age, but the evergreen favourites are popular with generation after generation. Among those shown here – all made by Chad Valley and mostly of British manufacture – tiddlywinks, magnetic fishing and the tailless donkey have all stood the test of time.*

Puzzles and Games

The most popular tests of manual dexterity in the 1930s were still the old-fashioned Chinese puzzles and maze boxes in which tiny silver balls had to be coaxed into different holes.

Children's card games and jigsaws had a long pedigree, but by the 1930s there was a much greater emphasis on fun.

Board games, too, were dominated by well-established models. There was, however, a growing taste for war games and new popular variants appeared, such as 'Aviation', 'Dover Patrol' and 'Tri-Tactics'.

The 1930s also saw the invention of 'Monopoly', the most famous of all board games. In the era of the Great Depression, its promise of spectacular wealth must have been the ultimate in wish-fulfilment for both children and adults alike.

Meccano kits were enormously popular. Bigger and better sets, incorporating pulleys, wheels and even motors, allowed elaborate working models to be made, providing an enjoyable introduction to practical mechanics.

▶ *Magnetic games were popular. Junior Spilli Wobble was a game of fun and dexterity.*

PRICE GUIDE ❷

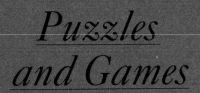

▲ *This old favourite is most collectable if it has all its pieces and its original box.*

PRICE GUIDE ❷

▶ *Paintings by Old Masters were a common subject for jigsaws.*

PRICE GUIDE ❷

◀▼ *Some games, such as table quoits, were sold as after-dinner games.*

PRICE GUIDE ❷

◀ *Coloured dominoes from the 1930s usually show wear but this set is in mint condition.*

PRICE GUIDE ❷

PRICE GUIDE

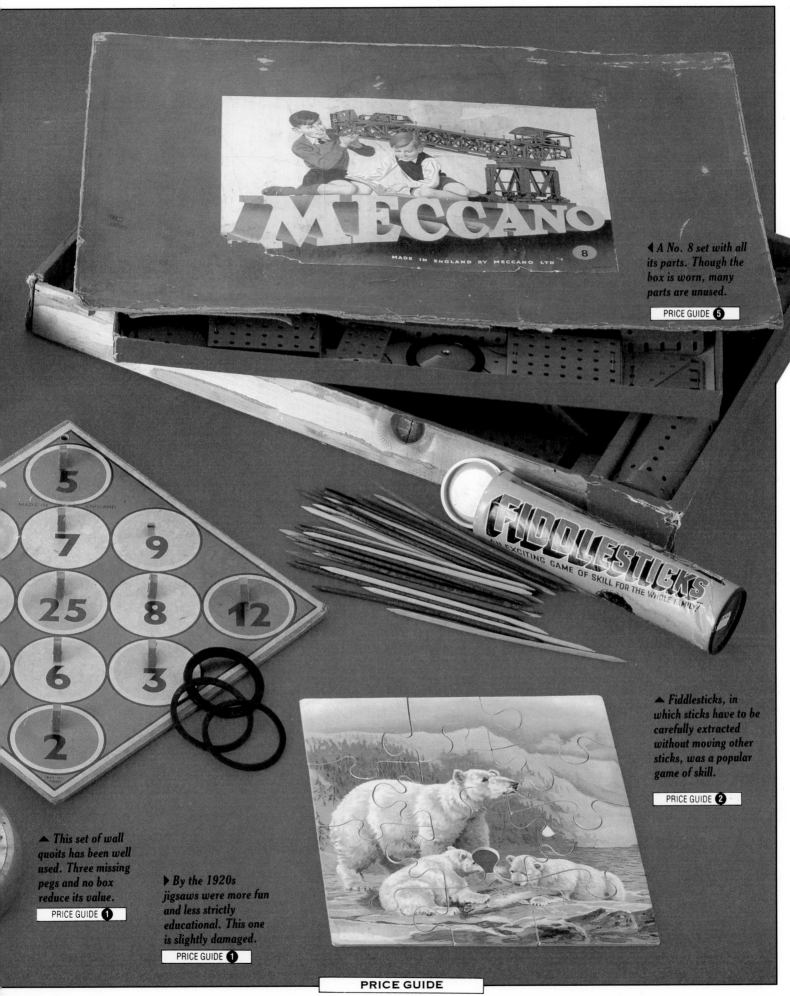

◀ A No. 8 set with all its parts. Though the box is worn, many parts are unused.

PRICE GUIDE ❺

▲ Fiddlesticks, in which sticks have to be carefully extracted without moving other sticks, was a popular game of skill.

PRICE GUIDE ❷

▲ This set of wall quoits has been well used. Three missing pegs and no box reduce its value.

PRICE GUIDE ❶

▶ By the 1920s jigsaws were more fun and less strictly educational. This one is slightly damaged.

PRICE GUIDE ❶

PRICE GUIDE

Soldiers, Cars and Planes

Model soldiers have a long history as playthings, but it was the English firm of William Britain which revolutionized the industry by devising the economical, hollow-cast process. The most collectable of Britain's soldiers date from their earliest period (1893-1914) but, with the topicality of re-armament during the 1930s, many new ranges were produced in the years preceding World War II.

Britain's were not alone in challenging the German dominance of the toy industry. In 1920, Frank Hornby, the inventor of Meccano, marketed his 'Hornby Train' in 0-gauge format. 'Hornby-Dublo', in 00-gauge, appeared in 1938. Although Hornby is probably best remembered for his train sets, he also turned his hand to other forms of transport – ships, planes and, eventually cars.

Made by the firm of Meccano, Hornby's Dinky toys first appeared in 1934, and are still being made today. Models from the 1930s are keenly sought after, particularly by American collectors and fetch extraordinary prices.

Tri-ang's Minic series of tinplate cars were larger than Dinky cars and included a clockwork motor, wound by a key. In surviving models the key is often missing and the motor is frequently defunct.

Clockwork motors were also a feature of many tin-plate model aircraft, enabling them to taxi along the floor. Planes sold as kits generally lack a motor. Well-made kit planes, particularly in wood, can be more attractive than the factory-made models.

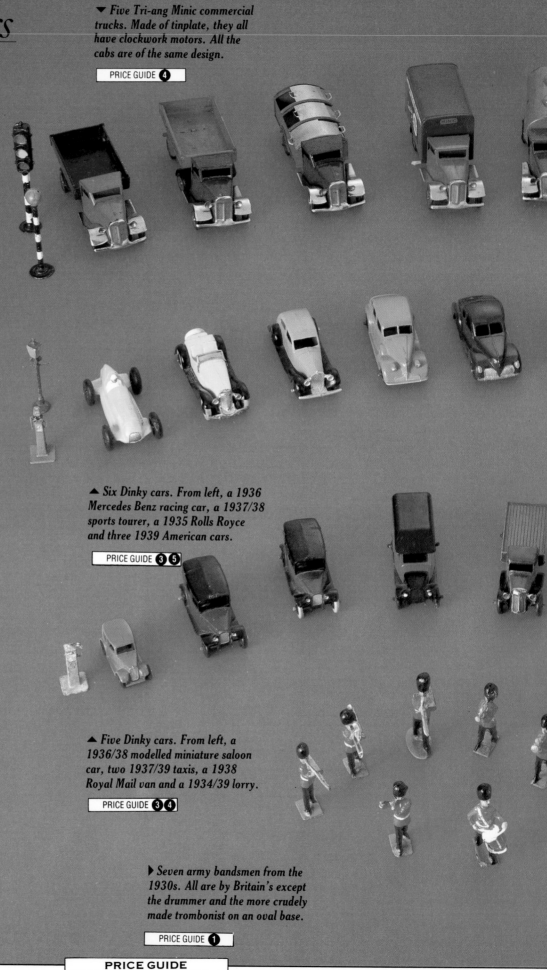

▼ *Five Tri-ang Minic commercial trucks. Made of tinplate, they all have clockwork motors. All the cabs are of the same design.*

PRICE GUIDE ❹

▲ *Six Dinky cars. From left, a 1936 Mercedes Benz racing car, a 1937/38 sports tourer, a 1935 Rolls Royce and three 1939 American cars.*

PRICE GUIDE ❸❺

▲ *Five Dinky cars. From left, a 1936/38 modelled miniature saloon car, two 1937/39 taxis, a 1938 Royal Mail van and a 1934/39 lorry.*

PRICE GUIDE ❸❹

▶ *Seven army bandsmen from the 1930s. All are by Britain's except the drummer and the more crudely made trombonist on an oval base.*

PRICE GUIDE ❶

PRICE GUIDE

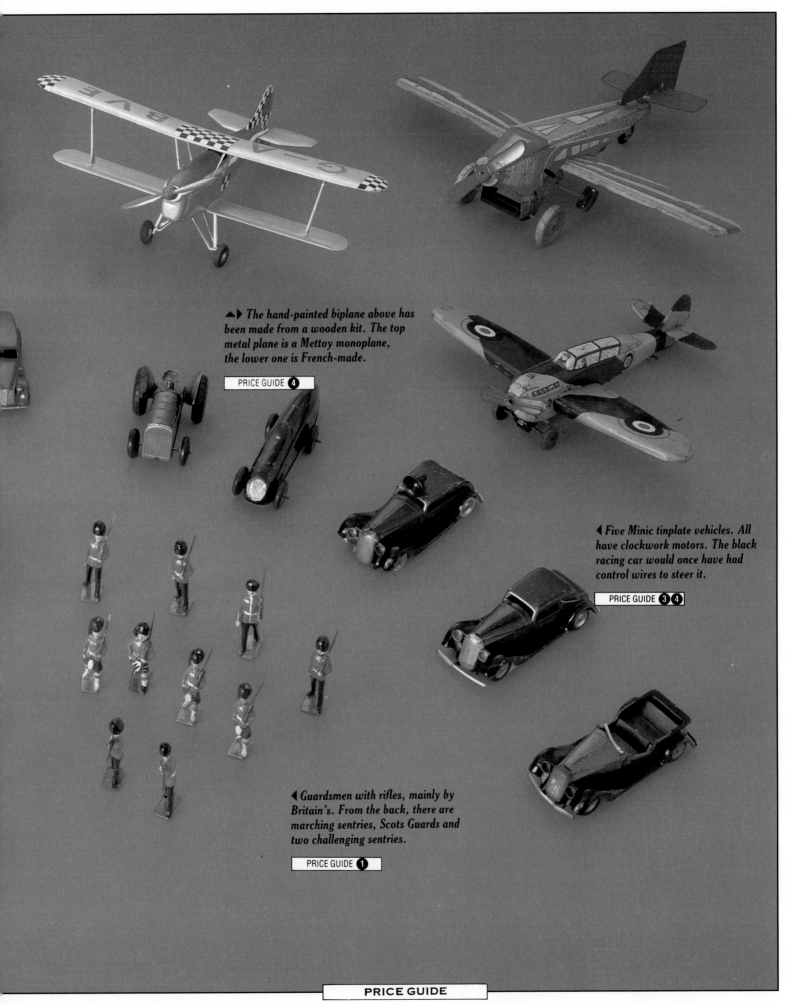

▲▶ *The hand-painted biplane above has been made from a wooden kit. The top metal plane is a Mettoy monoplane, the lower one is French-made.*

PRICE GUIDE **4**

◀ *Five Minic tinplate vehicles. All have clockwork motors. The black racing car would once have had control wires to steer it.*

PRICE GUIDE **3 4**

◀ *Guardsmen with rifles, mainly by Britain's. From the back, there are marching sentries, Scots Guards and two challenging sentries.*

PRICE GUIDE **1**

PRICE GUIDE

COLLECTOR'S TIPS

Though there is still room for the keen amateur collector, the upsurge of interest in toy collecting has pushed prices beyond the reach of many beginners.

Experienced collectors are usually in search of toys in mint condition. This is particularly true of toys from the 1920s

New and Old

BRITAIN'S ARE STILL MAKING TOY SOLDIERS. CURRENT MODELS (LEFT) ARE OF METAL BUT THEIR ACCESSORIES, SUCH AS RIFLES, ARE OF PLASTIC.

onwards, since many enthusiasts collect out of a nostalgia for their own childhood and are anxious to find items in their original packaging, complete with any ephemera, such as advertising material.

While this is the ideal, the reality is that metal toys were cheaply produced for a mass market and, though durable enough in the short term, they were not designed to last forever.

PROBLEM AREAS

The most common problems are metal fatigue and chipped paintwork. The former is most likely to affect toy soldiers, which were usually cast from an alloy of lead and tin. In other models, butthen mazak (a zinc alloy with aluminium, copper and magnesium) was usually employed, but this, too, can suffer from corrosion if impurities are present.

Metal affected by corrosion will have a grey, powdery surface and will be extremely brittle. The area most likely to be affected is the base, since the simpler casting procedure for this allowed a poorer quality metal to be used. Collectors are advised to avoid toys suffering from this condition and to protect

their own models by ensuring that they are not stored in a damp place.

Repainting is a matter of personal preference. Many enthusiasts enjoy restoring damaged models to resemble their original, colourful appearance, but serious collectors often find the results somewhat unnatural and this inevitably affects their market value. The same can be said of toys that have been restored. On model cars, for instance, tyres, headlamps and steering wheels of a later date may have been used to mask the loss of original features.

CONFUSING COPIES

Another familiar problem that confronts the beginner is that of identification. Many successful companies had their designs pirated by rivals and, in the early years of the century, almost identical copies of Britain's soldiers were being produced by firms such as Hanks and Renvoize. Britain responded by bringing a number of lawsuits and by printing on their boxes the firm stricture: 'Don't buy worthless copies of our English models. None genuine without our signature on box.'

To the modern enthusiast, these pirated

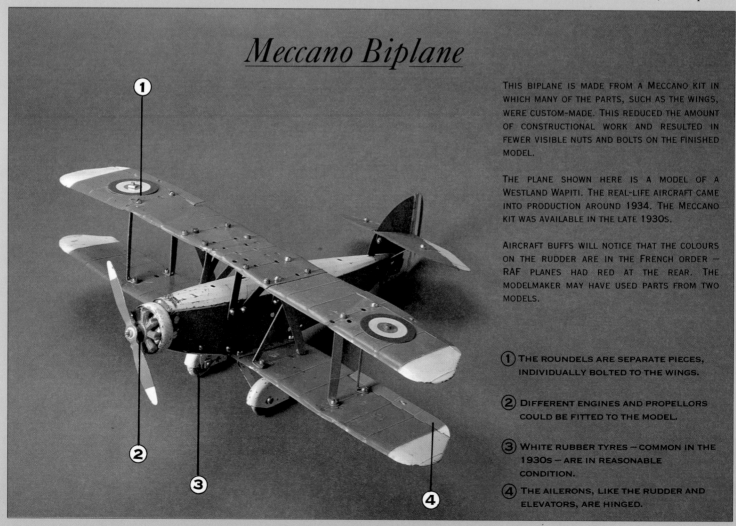

Meccano Biplane

THIS BIPLANE IS MADE FROM A MECCANO KIT IN WHICH MANY OF THE PARTS, SUCH AS THE WINGS, WERE CUSTOM-MADE. THIS REDUCED THE AMOUNT OF CONSTRUCTIONAL WORK AND RESULTED IN FEWER VISIBLE NUTS AND BOLTS ON THE FINISHED MODEL.

THE PLANE SHOWN HERE IS A MODEL OF A WESTLAND WAPITI. THE REAL-LIFE AIRCRAFT CAME INTO PRODUCTION AROUND 1934. THE MECCANO KIT WAS AVAILABLE IN THE LATE 1930S.

AIRCRAFT BUFFS WILL NOTICE THAT THE COLOURS ON THE RUDDER ARE IN THE FRENCH ORDER — RAF PLANES HAD RED AT THE REAR. THE MODELMAKER MAY HAVE USED PARTS FROM TWO MODELS.

① THE ROUNDELS ARE SEPARATE PIECES, INDIVIDUALLY BOLTED TO THE WINGS.

② DIFFERENT ENGINES AND PROPELLORS COULD BE FITTED TO THE MODEL.

③ WHITE RUBBER TYRES — COMMON IN THE 1930S — ARE IN REASONABLE CONDITION.

④ THE AILERONS, LIKE THE RUDDER AND ELEVATORS, ARE HINGED.

·CLOSE UP·

① REPLACEMENT TYRE

② FAIR WEAR AND TEAR

③ POST-WAR DINKY VAN

④ CLOCKWORK MOTOR

⑤ EARLY DINKY BASE

⑥ REPAIRED VEHICLE

① TYRES PERISH AND ARE OFTEN REPLACED. THE CUT ON THIS ONE IS VISIBLE.

② PAINT IS OFTEN WORN AWAY ON FACES AND OTHER PROMINENT PARTS.

③ IN POST-WAR MODEL VEHICLES THE WINDOWS WERE OFTEN NOT FILED OUT.

④ MOTORS ARE FREQUENTLY BROKEN. A UNIVERSAL KEY FITS THEM ALL.

⑤ THE OPEN-WORK CHASSIS IS TYPICAL OF EARLY MODELS, AS ARE WHITE TYRES.

⑥ FRONT FORKS HAVE BEEN SOLDERED AND THE AXLE AND WHEELS ARE NEW.

copies can often be as interesting as the original and some people hunt out the minor variations made by different companies and use this as a collecting theme.

Modern reproductions are a much greater problem. Usually, these were issued in good faith but, over the years, they have acquired a patina of age and can easily fool an unwary buyer. In the 1970s, for example, Meccano gave permission for some of the rarer Dinky cars to be reproduced in white metal, using a new rubber mould system. These reproductions can be identified by the absence of Meccano's trademark.

The beginner's best protection is to buy only from reputable dealers and to learn as much as possible from the literature available. In addition to modern guides, many original trade catalogues have been reprinted in recent years.

When it comes to displaying your collection it is comparatively easy to create interesting tableaux of toy soldiers, particularly as so many suitable accessories have been marketed. This is true of larger models, too, though lack of room can often preclude a permanent display and many enthusiasts prefer to keep their treasures carefully indexed and stored away in boxes. As in so many fields of collecting, the ideal solution is to have an abundance of space and a very understanding family.

POINTS TO WATCH

■ Retain all original boxes and packaging material. Do not attempt to repair these with sellotape.

■ Avoid metal toys suffering from corrosion. A rough, powdery surface is the telltale sign.

■ Beware of repainting, particularly where transfers are involved.

▶ *Celluloid clockwork acrobat. The flagged counterweight alters the acrobat's movements.*

Train Sets

To the delight of today's collector, train sets were often the one toy boys treated with love and respect, carefully returning trains and rails to their boxes after use

With a little prompting from their equally enthusiastic fathers, boys have always had a special relationship with their toy trains, whether they owned a splendid scenic layout in the loft or the most basic clockwork starter set. Some grew up to be model railway enthusiasts, demanding far greater attention to detail than is ever found on standard mass-produced toys. Most of us, however, can still wonder at the craftsmanship of old tinplate train sets, especially those made when the great steam locomotives they represented – the *Royal Scot* in its crimson L.M.S. livery or the *Flying Scotsman* in L.N.E.R. green – still thundered northwards out of Euston and King's Cross.

EARLY FLOOR-RUNNERS
Although toy trains were made in England, Germany and France shortly after the introduction of the railways, it was to be half a century before they were provided with any track to run on. Trains were soon available as 'penny' toys and by mid-Victorian times larger models were extremely popular as 'carpet toys'. Made either of wood or tinplate, these were simply pushed, or pulled on a string, across the floor. Their appeal depended on the variety of carriages and goods wagons that the locomotives pulled behind them. One of the most exciting presents a boy or girl could receive was a circus train, complete with caged lions and a big top to erect when the train reached its destination at the end of the corridor. Circus trains based on those of P. T. Barnum were especially popular in America. Some of these 'floor-runners' were equipped with automotive power, either clockwork, or more realistically, miniature steam engines. The first toy trains to be sold with track were probably brass steam locomotives or 'dribblers', as they became affectionately known. With the constant need to check the levels of water and oil and regulate the heat from the spirit lamp, running these highly educational steam-trains was far from child's play.

The first commercial company to produce a railway set that resembled the packages we buy today was Märklin, the great German toy firm based in Göppingen, which has maintained its place in the forefront of model railway engineering ever since. In the early 1890s their impressive figure-of-eight layouts for clockwork trains captured the public's imagination, showing for the first time the exciting possibilities of running one's own railroad. Despite the success of quaint antiques like Stephenson's *Rocket* and the *Adler* (Germany's first steam locomotive) Märklin and their eager competitors realized that what boys wanted for the nursery floor

was an approximate reconstruction of a modern railway system, complete with points, crossings, signals, gantries and all the more arcane paraphernalia of rail travel. Märklin's beautifully lithographed tinplate stations from their early ranges are highly-cherished objects, and sell for astronomical sums when in reasonable condition. Figures of station staff and other 'railway servants' were available to add a human touch to one's set, though in comparison with the trains these were usually a trifle oversized. The most important factor in the development of the industry was the range of straight and curved sectional rails, which enabled people bitten by the bug to expand their systems as far as their pockets and the space they had available would allow.

ON A SMALLER SCALE
One problem that needed to be solved quickly if chaos was to be avoided, was what scale these model railways ought to be. By the early years of this century, two major gauges (1 and 0) had been more or less standardized. The larger gauge 1 ran on track 45mm wide, the scale of the models being about 30:1. There were even larger gauges, used, for example, for the magnificent outdoor layouts in the palace gardens of Indian maharajahs, but nowadays gauge 1 is considered quite large enough for an outdoor display. The scale adopted by serious modellers and toy manufacturers for indoor layouts was, for the time being, a standard gauge 0, with

▼ *The appeal of model trains to today's collector is wide-ranging and includes, above all, early steam-driven and clockwork locomotives as well as electric trains and gaily-painted rolling stock.*

▲ *Märklin was renowned for its high-quality and inventive tinplate toys. Both the station building and the train are hand-painted, c.1900.*

rails 32mm apart, which represented a scale of 43:1.

Problems of scale were compounded by the fact that not all the world's railway ran on the standard gauge of 4ft 8½in (1.40m), but this was a matter for perfectionists. The degree of accuracy aspired to by Märklin and their slightly down-market rivals, Bing,

was remarkable, but they were always slightly shackled by the constraints of fitting standard clockwork motors or steam-engines to their locomotives. One manufacturer who determined that his trains should be near-perfect scale models of their prototypes was the Englishman, Wenman J. Bassett-Lowke, son of a Northampton engineer. Adopting many of the techniques of engineering in miniature pioneered by German craftsmen, he introduced his famous gauge 1 locomotive, the *Lady of the Lake* in 1901. Powered by steam, it was infinitely superior to anything that had been produced commercially in Britain before that date. The realism and detail of the *Lady of the Lake* and his first clockwork models, produced in 1904, forced even the great German manufacturers to look to their laurels. His showroom in High Holborn (opened in 1908) became as important a mecca for train-lovers (boys and grown men alike) as London's great railway terminals. Bassett-Lowke's business, conducted principally by mail order, was not limited to his own productions; he stocked a great many imported German models from Bing and other firms based in Nuremberg, among them the popular Bing Table Railway.

AN INTERNATIONAL EFFORT

So universal was the appeal of toy trains, that companies seldom limited themselves to making locomotives and rolling stock of their own national railway lines. A large company like Bing, which exported throughout the world, had to make models of the trains of every country in which they hoped to capture a share of the market. American locos, with their distinctive cow-catchers on the front, were obviously an exciting novelty to European children, who had never seen such things except in picture-books. Bing made a number of American locos, but the USA naturally had a large toy company of its own producing fine models to run on the new tin tracks. This was Ives of Bridgeport, an established firm, which produced many novelty floor trains, including ones that whistled and – with the help of a cigarette – expelled puffs of smoke as they ran.

The sources of power used on early train sets had obvious limitations: clockwork did not send a train very far, while steam was messy, causing blistered paintwork and burnt fingers. By 1898, Märklin were already experimenting with electricity, but early sets, running on a 120-volt supply straight from the mains, must have had a poor safety record and required strict parental supervision, if children were ever allowed to touch them. By the 1920s a number of systems were in operation, using transformers which reduced the current to 20 volts, but these were still fairly crude compared to modern power units which automatically vary the voltage to accelerate or decelerate the trains.

HORNBY TRAIN SETS

World War I not only brought the manufacture of toy trains to a temporary halt, when the fighting was over it also inhibited the formerly fruitful cooperation between British and German firms. One company to benefit from this was Hornby, already celebrated as the makers of Meccano. Hornby's plans to enter the toy train market just before the

War (using locomotives provided, it is thought, by Bing) had to be shelved. After the War they brought out clockwork trains 'put together on the Meccano principle', but they soon realized that true-to-life tinplate models were a much better bet. Their first boxed sets were relatively simple, containing engine, tender, two passenger cars and a set of rails, but by the end of the decade Hornby's range was so extensive that they could boast: 'The new accessories and rolling stock are of the latest types, all built in perfect proportion and all beautifully finished in correct colours ... The comprehensive range of Hornby rolling stock, accessories, rails, points and crossings enables a boy to duplicate almost every operation employed in modern railway practice.' The 1930s saw the production of many special high-quality models for their 20-volt system, while the splendid annual *Hornby Book of Trains* reinforced young boys' loyalty to a British-made product.

In the 1920s and 30s the market for train sets grew enormously, but the families buying them had rather less space in which the hobby could be pursued. Consequently manufacturers experimented with smaller gauges, which could provide a reasonable layout even on a table-top. H0 (half 0) was introduced in England by Bassett-Lowke, and the less satisfactory 00, first tried by German manufacturers, was taken up (in a slightly different form) by Hornby in 1938 with the well-known Dublo range. Locomotives for the smaller gauges would often be diecast, rather than constructed of printed tinplate, losing some of their old-world charm. Nevertheless almost all pre-war equipment is now keenly collected, and the encyclopaedic knowledge of real enthusiasts can be daunting to beginners in the field.

COLLECTABLE MODELS

Before the 1980s, old Hornby trains were somewhat despised by collectors, who were attracted by the superior craftsmanship of Märklin or Bassett-Lowke, but, as prices soared, people were forced to lower their expectations and explore the cheaper, homelier end of the market. Superior locomotives like the *Princess Elizabeth,* brought out in 1937 to be the flagship of the Hornby gauge 0 range, are very far from cheap, but assorted engines, rolling stock and accessories can still be found, without necessarily going to specialist sales.

Especially attractive are the colourful goods wagons advertising well-known products, although many of these date from the 50s. People's eyes are naturally drawn to the written word, so a wagon which boasts the inscription 'Fyffes bananas' or a coach which says 'Pullman' are always worth a great deal more than plain carriages or freight cars, provided, of course, that the paintwork is original. The livery of Hornby trains also affects their price; Southern Railway engines, for example, are much rarer than those of other companies. This applies to all makes of toy trains, and the relative rarity of a particular model in a particular livery has been thoroughly studied by the cognoscenti. As a particularly rare Märklin locomotive might cost many thousands of pounds, most people starting a collection will probably stick to humbler products like Hornby. There were, of course, other British companies making toy trains at the time, names like Chad Valley and Brimtoy, and one of their sets in good condition can sometimes be found at a less inflated price.

▲ *Although boxed train sets now fetch the highest prices, items bought individually or in lots at auction soon make up an interesting collection.*

The 1930s Girl's Room

A place to sleep, and to study, a young girl's bedroom contained her
most treasured possessions and expressed her unfolding personality

Ahome in the suburbs was the great dream for
parents of London children between the
wars. It would provide a place, close
enough to the city for father to travel to work, in
which children could blossom in 'air almost like that
of the country'. The model suburban 'villa' or semi-
detached had three or four bedrooms, two of which
were generally taken up by the children.

To the growing girl the suburbs meant a back
garden to play in (the front was kept as a show-
piece) and a room of her *very own,* unless she had the
bad luck to be burdened with an awful little sister!
Most middle-class incomes did not support a nanny
or full-time maid, and mother could only count on
day-help to bring order to the domestic chaos. Her
daughter, therefore, was responsible for the general
upkeep of her room; while it served as a place to
express her developing personality and to practise
her interests and hobbies, it also had to be easy to
keep clean and relatively tidy.

*For the first
time, girls of
the 1930s
were allowed
to express
personal taste
in furnishing
their own
rooms.*

129

Fitted carpets and highly-polished furniture were not for the young; floorboards were left bare and sealed or painted. Occasionally linoleum was preferred, since it was washable, though it was very cold to bare feet. In either case, the floor was partially covered by a large oblong throw-rug of Oriental or Axminster pattern.

▲ *This idealized illustration of a young girl enjoying breakfast in bed with her dolls is by Joyce Brisley, taken from* Blackie's Children's Annual.

PLAIN AND PRACTICAL

The furnishings of the room were also fairly spartan. Only the wallpaper and curtains lent an air of femininity to an older girl's room; younger children had eye-level friezes of nursery or fairytale characters by Kate Greenaway or Randolph Caldecott around their otherwise plain walls.

The furniture itself was usually of fumed oak or pine, the latter often painted white or a pastel shade, and sometimes decorated with transfer prints or painted scenes; Peter Rabbit in his cabbage patch was a particular favourite. As well as a chest of drawers and perhaps a small wardrobe for clothes, a bookcase, and a scaled-down table or chair for homework and play, there would also be a toy cupboard filled with toys and games.

▶ *An attractive effect can be achieved in a girl's bedroom using basic furniture. This simple decorative scheme gives a surprisingly homely effect.*

Bed frames would either be of enamelled iron or oak. Bunk beds, introduced on the domestic front after World War I, were particularly useful in homes where space was at a premium. So was born the classic childhood disagreement – who was to have the top bunk.

HEALTH AND VITALITY

By the 1930s it was not unusual to have a wash-basin fitted in a bedroom in place of the old-fashioned jug and bowl. It was more hygienic, more modern, and dispensed with the early-morning rush to the bathroom.

Well-ventilated rooms were seen as vital to health. Bedroom windows were left open at night and doors left ajar or fitted with ventilating panels. Another method of ensuring a constant current of air was a small cupboard built against an outside wall that was fitted with air vents. This cupboard kept milk, water and 'nursery refreshments' cool and sweet as well as encouraging the circulation of air.

The food-keeping properties of the cupboard were regularly tested, since frequent small snacks were thought to be good for children, particularly after strenuous activity, while studying, or just before bedtime. The magazines of the period are full of bright-eyed young women assuring anxious parents that they owed much of their evident health to Ovaltine and Ovaltine rusks. Other trusted stand-bys included Horlicks, ginger nuts, oat flapjacks and biscuits made from the newly-popular and exotic shredded coconut.

A GIRLISH GALLERY

Older girls would decorate their walls with pictures of matinée idols, film stars or their own heroes and heroines. Younger girls would probably have more 'suitable' pictures, supplied by mother or kindly aunts; perhaps a print of Millais' *Bubbles* or *The Piper of Dreams* by Estella Canziani. The choice was enormous; a little girl's bedroom could be a gallery of Victorian sentimental art, full of pretty children with plump, smiling faces and golden curls.

Religious pictures were not as popular as in earlier periods, but still found a home, especially if the

subjects were children, as with the old favourites, Millais' *Return of the Dove to the Ark* or *Christ in the Carpenter's Shop*. Though Holman Hunt's *Light of the World* did not show Christ as a child, it was perhaps the most popular of all childhood religious images.

The age of the sampler was not yet over, and many a young needlewoman would struggle away at a silk-thread cottage surrounded by ramrod-straight flowers. The completed work was invariably framed and afforded a place of honour on the bedroom wall. Mother might contribute more accomplished cross-stitch scenes, like those designed by Anne Orr that were offered in practically every issue of *Good*

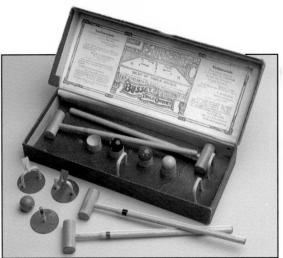

▶ *This miniature croquet set was specially designed by Bussey's to be played indoors on a table. Croquet was a popular game with girls, not least because it required less physical strength than many and gave them a fair chance to beat the boys. This table set made it possible to play in all weathers; even without a garden.*

Screen Idols

THE 1930s WAS THE GOLDEN AGE OF CINEMA. ALMOST HALF THE POPULATION OF BRITAIN WENT TO THE CINEMA EVERY WEEK. YOUNG GIRLS IDOLIZED THE STARS OF THE SCREEN THEY SAW ON SATURDAY MORNINGS AND AVIDLY FOLLOWED THE INTRICATES OF THEIR CAREERS AND PRIVATE LIVES.

JEAN HARLOW, THE 'BLONDE BOMBSHELL', AND GRETA GARBO WERE THE HEROINES OF OLDER GIRLS, WHILE THE MOST POPULAR MALE IDOLS WERE CARY GRANT AND LESLIE HOWARD, THE ALL-TIME FAVOURITE BEING CLARK GABLE.

Adolph Zukor Presents

CECIL B. DE MILLE'S "CLEOPATRA"

★ CLAUDETTE ★ WARREN ★ HENRY
COLBERT WILLIAM WILCOXON
A PARAMOUNT PICTURE

▲ *A shot from 'The Private Life of Don Juan' starring Douglas Fairbanks and Merle Oberon.*

◄ *Copies of the film-buff's bible of the 1930s, Filmgoer. with a popular game on the subject of film stars.*

◄ *A poster from 'Cleopatra', one of Cecil B. De Mille's popular epic pictures starring Claudette Colbert.*

131

Housekeeping in the early 1930s – fluffily-dressed ladies with cats, bonneted shepherdesses with gambolling lambs and similar confections.

FADS AND PASSIONS

Dance and horses were the abiding passions of the middle-class girl in the 1930s. Half the little girls in the country imagined themselves prima ballerinas in the making, their fantasies nurtured by Noel Streatfield's *Ballet Shoes,* published in 1936. Postcards and magazine illustrations of famous dancers like Pavlova and Alicia Markova joined the pictures of movie stars on the dresser mirror or over the chimney piece.

Others' fantasies revolved around riding. Few could afford their own pony, but riding stables thrived on young girls whose parents saved to give their child weekly lessons. Pictures of galloping steeds and elegant Arab heads were pinned up in her bedroom alongside the other heroes and heroines.

Pride of place on the bed was given to the girl's best doll, given when she was old enough to take care of her properly, say at 7 or 8, but still cherished when her owner was well into her teens. Some of the finest baby dolls date from this period, among them realistic 'sleeping' and 'laughing' babies.

Doll's hair was often worn in ringlets after the fashion of the child star, Shirley Temple, whose characteristic dimpled, smiling features appeared on many expensive dolls, as well as the paper dolls that enjoyed a vogue in the 1930s. Records for the new child-sized Victrola included Shirley warbling 'On the Good Ship Lollipop'.

Other period classics for the gramophone included 'Someday My Prince Will Come' and 'Hi-Ho, Hi-Ho' from Walt Disney's 1937 feature *Snow White and the Seven Dwarfs.* Disney's influence exceeded even Shirley Temple's. Mickey Mouse and Donald Duck were household names and by 1935 had become respectable enough for *Good Housekeeping* to feature them in a monthly cartoon page for young readers. Mickey and Minnie Mouse dolls

▲ *This rather modern-looking children's bedroom was actually designed in 1925 by Francis Jourdain for the French magazine* Intérieurs Français.

▼ *No young girl's bedroom was complete without a favourite doll, which was often treasured well into her teenage years.*

▲ *Some lucky children had a miniature Lloyd Loom chair in their bedroom, in which they could pore over their favourite books or comics.*

▶ *Like most young girls of today, a popular pastime for girls in the 1930s was playing games. These may have been bought by a favourite Uncle as a birthday or Christmas present. 'Next Line Please' was often played at parties; the participants were given the beginning line of a nursery rhyme and had to recite the next line.*

were sold in very large numbers during the 1930s.

After 1927, education was reorganized according to the recommendations of the Hadow report. Elementary education (to age 11) was entrusted to primary schools, while 'modern schools' took the child on to leaving age, 14 in the 1930s. More girls were encouraged to stay on and continue their education, with a view to correcting the imbalance in university admissions.

The new emphasis on learning was reflected in the introduction of homework and in the use of study tables and desks in the bedroom. Like the more traditional bedroom furniture, these were usually of polished pine or fumed or honey oak.

Books for children became an important priority for many publishers. School stories and historical romances attempted to teach everyday ethics and facts in ways which were appealing to children. The introduction of the battery-powered electric torch to the domestic market in the 1920s made it possible to read these gripping yarns – and the less-approved comics – under the covers, and another classic childhood pattern was established for years to come.

LIFE AND LEISURE

Good Reading

THE 1930S WAS AN ERA WHEN CHILDREN WERE ENCOURAGED TO READ AS NEVER BEFORE. MAGAZINE ARTICLES TRIED TO STEER THE RESPONSIBLE PARENT TOWARDS TRIED AND TRUSTED BOOKS WHICH WOULD DEVELOP THEIR CHILDREN'S READING ABILITY AND CHARACTER. SUCH WELL-MEANING DIRECTIVES USUALLY CONCENTRATED ON ACKNOWLEDGED CLASSICS LIKE *THE WIND IN THE WILLOWS* OR *TREASURE ISLAND*.

MANY OF THE MOST LOVED CHILDREN'S BOOKS, HOWEVER, DID NOT FIT INTO THIS SAFE MOULD. *SWALLOWS AND AMAZONS*, FIRST PUBLISHED IN 1930, WAS A VERY SLOW STARTER AND WAS NOT REALLY POPULAR UNTIL THE 1940S. THE TOYTOWN BOOKS ONLY BECAME POPULAR AFTER THEIR RENDITION ON RADIO IN CHILDREN'S HOUR FROM 1929. FOUR REAL CHILDHOOD CLASSICS SAW THE LIGHT OF DAY IN THE 1930S: JOHN MANSFIELD'S *THE BOX OF DELIGHTS* (1935), P. L. TRAVER'S *MARY POPPINS* (1934) AND J. R. R. TOLKIEN'S *THE HOBBIT* (1937). ONE OF THE GREATEST OF ALL CHILDREN'S BOOKS *WINNIE THE POOH*, AND ITS SEQUEL *THE HOUSE AT POOH CORNER* WERE WRITTEN BY A. A. MILNE IN 1926 AND 1928, ALTHOUGH THEIR POPULARITY CONTINUED THROUGHOUT THE 1930S AND TO THE PRESENT DAY.

▶ A SELECTION OF THE MOST POPULAR GIRLS' BOOKS FROM THE 1930S, INCLUDING THE *OXFORD ANNUAL FOR GIRLS*, ONE OF A NUMBER OF ANNUALS PUBLISHED SPECIFICALLY FOR GIRLS TO RIVAL THOSE PUBLISHED FOR BOYS. ALL CHILDREN'S ANNUALS, ESPECIALLY PRE-WAR PUBLICATIONS, ARE NOW AVIDLY COLLECTED ALONG WITH MOST EARLY BOOKS.

Children's China

China made especially for children was popular during the inter-war
years. Children's crockery and bedroom ornaments
have now become collectable

From toothbrush holders to teapots, the range of china made for youngsters during the inter-war years was considerable. A little girl could eat her breakfast, lunch and dinner off her own set of crockery. On a rainy afternoon she could have her friends around for tea, served, with Mother's help, off a special tea set. And at the end of the day she could go off to bed with her favourite china ornaments by her bedside.

FIRST STEPS
The pieces we think of now as children's china tend mainly to be those used by children of toddler age upwards, but the earliest examples were intended for infants.

In the 18th century, numerous potteries were turning out baby-orientated items – Spode made a baby's cup shaped like a duck and a Bristol Delftware feeding bottle was made to look like a Chinaman.

Pottery feeding bottles of the early 19th century were made of earthenware, and were beautifully decorated in blue underglaze printing with pastoral scenes, romantic views of ruined castles, floral designs or coloured spots and stars. The bottles were boat shaped, with a spout for baby to suck.

During the Victorian era, parents began to take an interest in educating their

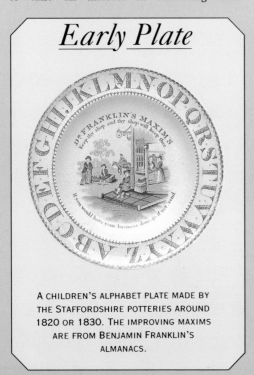

Early Plate

A CHILDREN'S ALPHABET PLATE MADE BY
THE STAFFORDSHIRE POTTERIES AROUND
1820 OR 1830. THE IMPROVING MAXIMS
ARE FROM BENJAMIN FRANKLIN'S
ALMANACS.

children, and nursery china illustrated with nursery rhymes and worthy advice came on to the market. Few pieces had a maker's mark and most were printed in monochrome sepia, black or blue. Some were decorated with animals or flowers in relief.

NEW STYLES

By the early 20th century, children's china had taken on its modern form. Earthenware had been largely replaced by lighter, harder-wearing bone china, and monochrome decoration had given way to bright colours. Relief decoration, which was attractive but difficult to keep clean, had become quite rare. Popular children's characters, from Mabel Lucie Attwell's elves to cinema cartoon figures, featured strongly. Children's china had become fun.

A tea set featuring characters from *Alice in Wonderland,* which Royal Doulton had been making since 1906, was still available in the early 1930s. Attractively fluted at the top, the teacup had 'Alice and the caterpillar' printed on one side within a framework of twining leaves, and on the opposite side appeared the legend 'Repeat, "You are old Father William", said the caterpillar'.

BUNNYKINS

This set had ceased production by the end of the 1930s, as had all Royal Doulton's other children's lines, because in 1934 a design was introduced which was to become popular enough to supersede them all – Bunnykins.

The artist behind Bunnykins was Sister Mary Barbara, a nun who taught history at a convent school. Christened Barbara Vernon Bailey, she was the daughter of Cuthbert Bailey, who became general manager of Royal Doulton at Burslem in 1925. He was looking for new designs for nursery ware, and his daughter's 'doodles' of playful rabbits came to mind.

The 'Barbara Vernon' characters, among which her father sometimes featured as an older rabbit with round glasses and a pipe, are still used, essentially unaltered, today. By the Second World War there were 66 different Bunnykins scenes decorating plates, cups, sugar bowls, jam pots and other crockery.

In addition to Royal Doulton, the other major potteries making children's china were Wedgwood and Shelley, and smaller makers abounded. Although many designers were anonymous, including the designer of the successful Royal Doulton 'Alice in Wonderland' line, well-known designers were credited. Shelley used Mabel Lucie Attwell's designs, and Susie Cooper drew the simple but dynamic animals and toy characters which decorated Wedgwood's 'Nursery Ware for the Discriminating Juvenile' series. Kate Greenaway's designs, popular with the Victorians, were still being turned out by a number of makers. Walt Disney was credited on a Wadeheath tea set featuring his characters.

NIGHT LIGHTS AND TOILET SETS

Though crockery was the dominant type of children's china, there were other items too. In the bedroom, were little pottery animals and china bookends and nightlights. For the bathroom, toilet ware was sold by Heal's. Their 'Poole Pottery Toilet Set' carried a cheerful cock crowing on the ewer and basin in soft shades of red, green and blue on a cream ground. There was also a soap dish, toothbrush vase and a sponge bowl in the set. Children's miniature china of the period includes doll's-house tea sets and birthday and Christmas cake decorations. Many of the latter were German in origin and featured Santa Claus in a surprising variety of poses, even riding an elephant.

◀ *The main feature of children's crockery is the attractive illustrations. Many come from children's fiction, nursery rhymes or cartoon films but others – such as Eric Ravilious' Alphabet bowl – are original designs. Animal ornaments can enhance a collection.*

▶ *A 1937 publicity leaflet for Bunnykins nursery ware. The range was produced in earthenware and bone china from Barbara Vernon's sketches.*

Bedroom Ornaments

China ornaments graced many a girlish bedroom in the 1930s. At their simplest, they might be inexpensive miniature cradles that were produced for Christening cakes and were kept and displayed as mementoes on the mantelpiece.

Much more extravagant were the little figures made by Royal Doulton, including a series designed by Arthur Leslie Harradine called 'Tinkle Bell', 'Dinky Doo', 'Babie' and 'Tootles', all of them bonneted and in long pastel dresses, and all less than 5″ tall. Royal Doulton also made nursery-rhyme figures such as Little Jack Horner.

Although not strictly children's china, Sylvac ware, made by Shaw and Copestake and first introduced in the late 1930s, found its way into many childish hearts – and bedrooms. The Sylvac range features endearing little dogs, their heads cocked to one side enquiringly, as well as less lifelike cats and highly-stylized rabbits, which are quite Deco in appearance. These earthenware pieces came in pale green, buff, blue and occasionally yellow.

The bedtime story may have come from a book standing between china bookends, and even after lights out the little girl did not have to lose touch altogether with her china friends. Royal Doulton made a Bunnykins night-light – a bunny undoing his braces – while several of the Staffordshire potteries made china cottage nightlights which glimmered comfortingly in the dark.

▼ *A soulful-looking ceramic setter's head in a ring, forming a wall plaque.*

PRICE GUIDE **2**

▼ *Two Sylvac terriers in green and buff, with heads characteristically to one side.*

PRICE GUIDE **3**

▼ *A typically alert fox terrier made by Shaw and Copestake in the 1930s.*

PRICE GUIDE **2**

▼ *Two ceramic bookends by a German manufacturer. They depict a boy with a posy and a girl with a book. Both children are in 18th-century costume.*

PRICE GUIDE **3**

▲ *A Sylvac button tidy in two colours. Impressed underneath is the Sylvac backstamp.*

PRICE GUIDE **2**

PRICE GUIDE

▼ *Two Sylvac rabbits in subtly different styles – note the herringbone pattern on the green bunny's ears.*

PRICE GUIDE ❶

▼ *Two long-necked cartoon dogs. Part of the Sylvac range, they are made by Shaw and Copestake.*

PRICE GUIDE ❷

◄ *A ceramic money box in the shape of a rabbit. The nose, eyes and claws are hand-painted.*

PRICE GUIDE ❷

▼ *Two ceramic figures on alabaster bookends. One girl holds a camera, the other a rose.*

PRICE GUIDE ❷

◄ *A white and tortoiseshell cat with green eyes. One of the Sylvac series, it dates from the 1930s.*

PRICE GUIDE ❸

PRICE GUIDE

Children's Crockery

Children's crockery came in large sets in the 19th century, but by the 1930s the tendency for smaller families was reflected in children's china. Crockery would often be bought in place settings rather than in huge sets. The size of pieces was variable. Some cups were virtually full sized, whilst others were plainly made for little hands.

Boxed tea sets, accompanied by silver teaspoons, were produced as Christening presents. Sometimes, these were treasured but never used and can still be found in near-mint condition.

Royal Doulton's nursery rhyme and Bunnykins patterns, Shelley's Mabel Lucie Attwell and Heathcote's very up-to-date 'Wireless' design were foremost among the multitude of styles available. Wedgwood managed to combine the traditional and the contemporary in one piece. Daisy Makeig-Jones took the 'Willow' pattern in 1926 and superimposed playful paintings of fairyland figures in orange, green and pink.

The 'Willow' pattern was underglaze printed in blue, but most children's crockery was transfer-printed in bright colours on top of the glaze, though some featured printed outlines which were painted in.

▶ *A soup plate with Mabel Lucie Attwell designs, showing a baby in a caravan with elves and animals. Her rhymes are distinctive.*

PRICE GUIDE ❸

▶ *A porcelain children's beaker from the Simple Simon nursery tea service, first produced by Royal Doulton in 1920.*

PRICE GUIDE ❷

▼ *A mug and a plate, part of a place setting, with 'Your Licence Please' illustrations.*

PRICE GUIDE ❷

▶ *A porridge bowl, plate and two egg cups in the Bunnykins series. The plate, which has Barbara Vernon's facsimile signature, shows a Bunnykins Santa Claus.*

PRICE GUIDE ❸

PRICE GUIDE

◄ *A cup and plate from the 'Alice in Wonderland' tea set by Royal Doulton, after Tenniel's drawings.*

PRICE GUIDE **3**

▼ *Three pieces from designs by Heath Robinson.*

PRICE GUIDE **5**

▼ *A black and white nursery rhyme jug made from 1907 until 1934.*

PRICE GUIDE **3**

▼ *A mug which was produced from 1903 to 1939. It illustrates the 'Old Mother Hubbard' nursery rhyme.*

PRICE GUIDE **3**

► *A nursery rhyme mug designed by Ann Anderson.*

PRICE GUIDE **3**

▲ *A child's pusher, spoon and fork in electroplated nickel silver. A popular christening present.*

PRICE GUIDE **1**

▲ *A mug in the Christopher Robin series by Ashtead Potters from E. H. Shepard's drawings.*

PRICE GUIDE **4**

▲ *A Paragon bowl featuring Mickey Mouse and Minnie at the piano.*

PRICE GUIDE **3**

PRICE GUIDE

COLLECTOR'S TIPS

The quantities in which children's china was produced in the 1930s makes starting a collection a relatively easy matter. Collecting at random, however, is rarely satisfying, and most people specialize, collecting either the work of a single factory, like Doulton, a particular designer, such as Mabel Lucie Attwell or Barbara Vernon, one type of ware, such as teapots or nightlights or some other theme – frogs, for instance, or characters from Disney films.

CHOOSING A SPECIALISM

The most collectable factories are the famous, 'aristocratic' ones like Royal Doulton and Wedgwood. These offer an enormous amount of scope in the number of designs produced, but the problem for the small collector is that the children's china market here overlaps with the interests of mainstream factory collectors and prices can get rather high.

Royal Doulton figures, for example, are much sought after by collectors, particularly in the USA, and as a result some childhood figures can fetch several hundred pounds. Conversely, Sylvac, for example, is not widely collected and the firm remains largely unknown outside the specialist children's china field. As a result most of its products

COMPARISONS

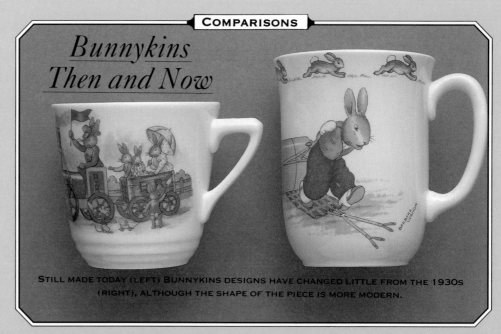

Bunnykins Then and Now

STILL MADE TODAY (LEFT) BUNNYKINS DESIGNS HAVE CHANGED LITTLE FROM THE 1930S (RIGHT), ALTHOUGH THE SHAPE OF THE PIECE IS MORE MODERN.

can easily be bought for a few pounds.

Famous designer's names also push up prices. Names like Eric Ravilious, Mabel Lucie Attwell and Leslie Harradine are eminently collectable. The Ravilious alphabet mug, for example, costs four times as much as a similar Royal Doulton nursery

rhyme mug by an anonymous designer. The children's tea sets made by Clarice Cliff are no less sought after than her other work.

Teapots are always collectable. The Bunnykins teapot, in the shape of a rabbit, is one of the most expensive pieces of children's china. Close behind is the duck-

Baby's Plate by Mabel Lucie Attwell

THE BABY'S PLATE IS A PIECE OF CHINA CUSTOM-DESIGNED FOR YOUNG CHILDREN. IT IS HEAVY SO THAT IT WON'T SLIDE AROUND THE TABLE AND CAN'T BE THROWN OFF EASILY. IT IS ALSO STRONG SO THAT IF IT IS THROWN OFF IT IS LESS LIKELY TO BREAK. THE LIP ON THE INSIDE OF THE RIM IS DESIGNED TO PUSH FOOD ON TO THE SPOON AND TO MAKE IT LESS EASY FOR THE SPOON TO SHOVEL FOOD OVER THE EDGE.

MABEL LUCIE ATTWELL DESIGNED HER NURSERY TEA SERVICE FEATURING LITTLE ELVES – THE BOO-BOOS – IN 1926. IT WAS MANUFACTURED BY THE SHELLEY POTTERY.

① THE LIPPED RIM PUSHES FOOD ON TO A SPOON.

② EACH PIECE HAS A LITTLE RHYME PRINTED ON IT.

③ THE ELVES WERE CREATED BY MABEL LUCIE ATTWELL.

④ ALL PIECES FEATURE THE DESIGNER'S SIGNATURE.

FAIRY FOLK WITH TINY WINGS PLAYING ALL OVER THE PLATES AND THINGS'

MABEL LUCIE ATTWELL

BABY'S PLATE

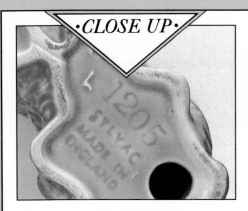

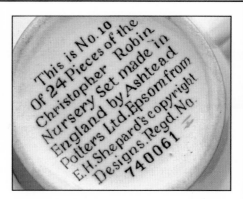

① IMPRESSED BACKSTAMP

② BUNNYKINS BACKSTAMP

③ BACKSTAMP

① BEFORE 1946 THE BACKSTAMP SAID 'SYLVAC SEMI-PORCELAIN'.

② THE BUNNYKINS BACKSTAMP DESIGNED BY HUBERT LIGHT FOR ROYAL DOULTON.

③ ASHTEAD POTTERS' BACKSTAMP GIVES FULL DETAILS ON THIS SET.

④ TRANSFER-PRINTED DESIGN ON A GOOSEY, GOOSEY, GANDER PLATE.

⑤ HAND-PAINTED PIED PIPER DESIGN ON A CHRISTIAN-NAME MUG.

④ PRINTED DESIGN

⑤ HAND-PAINTED DESIGN

shaped teapot and accompanying jug and sugar bowl designed by Mabel Lucie Attwell for Shelley around 1930.

The Bunnykins series, still being added to today, is one of the most popular themes for a collection. Barbara Vernon's drawings were adapted for transfer printing by Royal Doulton's Hubert Light. It was he who introduced the chain of rabbits chasing one another around the rim that has become the trademark of the line and it was he who introduced the backstamp of three red-jacketed bunnies below the Doulton mark. Pieces from the 1930s can be recognized by the facsimile Barbara Vernon signature in blue that appears on them.

RARITY VALUE

Collectors have ensured that some pieces – often the least regarded when originally manufactured – have become more valued than others. Egg-cups, for instance, tend to be more valued than other tea-set items, while night-lights, candle-holders and napkin rings also have rarity value.

Many items were originally sold in sets. Complete sets, however, do not turn up often as they were subject to loss and breakage. When they do – often after having been given as christening presents and carefully treasured ever since – up to 50 per cent can be added to the cost of the individual items bought separately. The

addition of the original presentation box will push this up even further.

Despite their escalating value, few pieces are known to have been faked on a large scale. Good forgeries can be virtually indistinguishable from the real thing and the best advice is to beware of low prices for rare items and to seek expert advice before investing in any high-priced piece.

BUYING CHILDREN'S CHINA

There are a few shops specializing in children's china, but perhaps the best hunting ground for the aspiring collector is the odd lot at the country auction, the car boot sale or an antiques shop. Children's china is a secondary line for many shops, but most will have a few pieces.

Children's tableware, by its very nature, has usually been subjected to some hard use, so when buying pay particular care that there are no chips, cracks or scratches, that any transfer printing has not been rubbed or marked, and that the maker's mark is cleanly struck and easy to read. Some earlier pieces were hand-enamelled over the glaze, and this is particularly prone to chipping.

▶ *Eric Ravilious' Alphabet design was executed for Wedgwood and appeared on a range of children's china. Interestingly, the letters 'YZ' appear inside the mug.*

POINTS TO WATCH

■ Repairs show up in variations in the colour, body or glaze caused by the repair materials being softer than the original and fired at lower temperatures.

■ Glaze may crackle after long use, and this does not detract over-much from value.

■ Cracks and chips *do* detract from value.

■ Familiarize yourself with the field by reading books and auction catalogues then follow your instincts when buying.

INDEX

INDEX

143

PICTURE CREDITS

Pictures on pages 23(bl, br), 29, 71(t) by Gracious Permission of Her Majesty The Queen. Beamish Museum: 42(br), 47(t). Bridgeman Art Library: 10(br) S.J. Philips, 11(bl) City of York Art Gallery, 16/7 Bethnall Green Museum, London, 17 Bethnall Green Museum, London, 20(t) Rotunda Dolls House Museum, Oxford, 26 Christies, London, 26/7 Christies, London, 28 Raphael Vals Gallery, London, 42/3, 43(bl), 45, 66(t,bl), 67(t,cl,b), 68(t,cl,br), 68/9(b), 70/1, 74, 75, 76/7, 78/9, 80/1, 90, 102(b), 103(t), 106, 106/7, 108/9(b), 115(b). Christies Colour Library: 11(br), 12(tl), 16. Deeley Photographic Services: 41. Design Council: 119. Ray Duns: 24(t), 25, 27(t,c), 28/9, 33(1), 49, 51(b), 56/7, 58/9 Jessop Classic Photographic Equipment, 60/1 Jessop Classic Photographic Equipment, 98(bl), 99(t,bl), 100(tr), 101(t), 103(r), 104/5, 107, 131(t), 131(br), 132, 133, 134. Andrew Edwards: 82. E.T. Archive: 132(t). Mary Evans Photographic Library: 13(c,bl,br), 60(t), 68(cr), 69(b), 98(br), 99(br), 100(b), 101(c), 116(c), 116(c), 130(t). Fine Art Photographic: 43(br), 44, 45(b), 46/7, 62, 90/1, 92(t), 98(t), 100(tl), 101(b), 102/103, 104(t), 108/9(t). Christine Hanscombe: 66(br). Syd Hughes: 38/9, 39, 40, 50/1, 52/3, 54/5. Hulton Deutsch Collection: 42(bl), 112(t), 116(t), 117(c). Kobal Collection: 131(bl,cr). Lauros-Giraudon: 22. Ranald Mackechnie: 10/1, 13(t), 14/5, 31, 134/5, 136/7, 138/9, 140(t,b), 141(t). Mansell Collection: 67(cr). Marshall Arts: 50. Michael Michaels: 120/1, 122/3, 124, 125, 126(b), 128(t). Museum of London: 20(b). The National Trust: 10(tl) John Bethell, 14/5 Mark Fiennes, 19(t,b), 97. The National Trust for Scotland: 8/9. Ian O'leary: 62/3, 64, 74/5. Philips Fine Art Auctioneers: 18(t), 21(b), 126(t). Popperfoto: 63. Colin Putbrace from R.C. Bell Collection: 32/3. Peter Reilly: 72/3, 92(b), 93. Royal Borough of Kensington and Chelsea Library and Arts Service: 10/1(b). courtesy Royal Doulton: 135. Duncan Smith: 94, 96. Jessica Strang: 15. Victoria and Albert Museum, London: 12(tr, b), 18(b), 30, 33. Josiah Wedgwood & Sons Ltd: 141(b). Rosemary Weller: 82/3, 84, 85, 86, 87, 91. Elizabeth Whiting & Associates: 23(t), 35(t), 47(b), 51(t), 65, 70, 114.

Some of this material has previously appeared in the partwork Times Past.